8 Ways to Mind Your Own Business

Clara Rose
Debbie Clement-Large

Rose & Clement-Large

Copyright © 2020 Clara Rose & Debbie Clement-Large

All rights reserved. No portion of this book may be reproduced, stored in a retrieval system, or transmitted in any form or by any means; electronic, mechanical, photocopy, recording, scanning, or other, except for brief quotations in critical reviews or articles, without the prior written permission of the authors.

Published by RoseDale Publishing AND Whole Hearted Books

ISBN: 978-1-7344263-3-5 (US)
ISBN: 978-1-8381106-0-4 (UK)

Dedication

To Steve, Mae, and Mum, who always believed in me. - Debbie

To Larry, my husband and friend, who is my biggest fan and supporter. - Clara

Rose & Clement-Large

Table of Contents

Dedication iii

Acknowledgments 1

Preface 3

1st Way 7

    Passion MATTERS 9

    Inspired Passion 21

2nd Way 35

    Creation MATTERS 37

    Inspired Creation 47

3rd Way...63

    Business MATTERS 65

    Inspired Business 73

4th Way 87

    Operation MATTERS 89

    Inspired Operations 97

5th Way 109

    Prosperity MATTERS 111

    Inspired Prosperity 119

6th Way 133

    Connection MATTERS 135

    Inspired Connection 143

7th Way 155

    Customer MATTERS 157

    Inspired Customer 165

8th Way 175

    Employee MATTERS 177

    Inspired Employee 187

8 Inspired Ways that MATTER 201

Inspired Afterword 213

About Clara Rose 215

About Debbie Clement-Large 217

Acknowledgments

To the wonderful members of our mastermind group, *The Business Support Network*, where we met, thank you for being a part of this journey.

Rose & Clement-Large

Preface

This book is for those who dare to be truth seekers. Those who know-deep down there is a yearning for their work to be a creative expression of who they really are. To be the creator of their own journey. To make their own rules in which they earn their financial prosperity on their own terms. Does this sound like you? Are you ready to step out of the shadows and to take up your rightful place as the owner of your own destiny? Are you ready to start your own business?

Being an entrepreneur is not for the fainthearted, but it does provide you with a wonderful opportunity to be of service, in the way that feels right for you. You will be the Captain of your own ship and can guide it in the direction of fulfilling your passion in life. As you embark upon your adventure, you will discover in this book, 8 ways to help you navigate your journey.

Having been both an entrepreneur and business coach for many years, mainly in the service industries, Clara Rose will share with you the nuts and bolts needed to get your own business off the ground. This know-how is invaluable, and her 8 ways will take you on a journey through the necessary steps to launch successfully. She educates you about developing your strategic plan and undertaking due diligence on your idea, creating your brand, setting up the structure, as well as the systems and processes of your business, and thinking about budgeting. Clara also covers the important topics for building your audience of raving fans, growing your business, and taking on employees. These are lessons steeped in years of experience, which will help you avoid many of the mistakes or wasted time that can happen when setting off on our own entrepreneurial journey.

Knowing the why, wherefore, and how, to is so important when starting a new business, but many step by step guides don't cover the aligning of your attitude and mind-set to support your new endeavour. This book is different.

As with any journey you embark on, you will want to compare where you are now, to your desired destination. Taking action, by *doing,* is one thing, but if your beliefs or thinking aren't fully supporting your journey, you could end up making a U-turn, or hitting an iceberg and sinking. We can be incredibly good at unconsciously getting in our own way, and self-sabotaging our success. It is for this reason, each nuts and bolts chapter is accompanied by an *inspired way* to align your thoughts and beliefs, to support your intentions at each step of your journey.

Debbie will gently and lovingly guide you through the mental minefield, as you discover whether your mind-set is supporting or unconsciously sabotaging your journey. She not only runs her own internationally recognised, award winning coaching practice, but also coached corporately for several years within the transformation and change arena, on multi-million-pound projects. Debbie passionately believes that no matter where you are now, it is never too late to positively change your life, for if she can do it, you can too.

As you read both the strategy and the mind-set chapters, you may notice some seeming inconsistencies with the spellings. These are intentional. Clara is based in the US, and Debbie is based in the UK. To remain true to their voices, they have used the correct spellings for their part of the world. One version, or other, will resonate with you, depending on where you are in the world.

Clara Rose and Debbie are delighted to share their own journeys with you in this book, to help illuminate your way. With both the practical steps and the loving attitudinal healing support you'll receive, you will be destined to create the right business, in the right way, that will support you for as long as you wish.

From the Authors

We are enjoying our own journeys, and we know you will too. In our experience, when you set sail on your own business adventure, you never look back.

Clara Rose
Debbie Clement-Large

Rose & Clement-Large

8 Ways to Mind Your Own Business

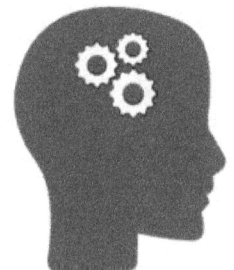 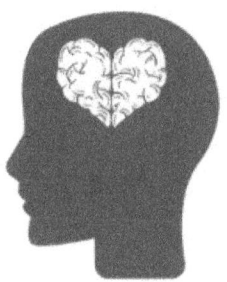

1ˢᵗ Way

Passion MATTERS

Many people dream of working for themselves. They envision a schedule that allows time freedom and flexibility, and of course a steady flow of revenue to make all their dreams come true. It all sounds so amazing, and it really can be, but any business owner will tell you… the reality of the day to day, is often very different from their original vision.

For some people, the desire to launch their own business stems from a sense of dissatisfaction in their current career path. For other people it might come from an unreasonable boss, or it might be the work itself, causing a lack of fulfillment in their current situation. Whatever the reason, the allure of business ownership can be compelling.

Certain people, much like myself, grew up knowing they wanted to be self-employed. Perhaps they had a parent or family member who modeled it for them. My father was self-employed, and it shaped my perception about business ownership. I witnessed the long hours and hard work, but I also recognized the value of calling your own shots!

Whatever YOUR reason for starting this journey; you've made the decision to start your own business, to take the plunge and finally work for yourself. That is probably why you are here today, learning about mindset and strategies for the business start-up.

Now, you've probably heard an expert or influencer say that you need to find your passion. While I do agree, you should feel passionate about your new endeavor, I'd like to suggest there is something more. It's not enough to feel a passion for the products or services your new business will offer. Yes, passion matters, but it's not enough on its own.

For many years I've worked with entrepreneurs and business owners, at all stages of their business. I've consulted on every topic imaginable, that's related to business. What kind of business to start, how to start a business, how to set up systems and processes, strategic planning for launching or growing a business, the best ways to expand influence to generate more business leads, content strategy around articles or books, becoming a published author to gain more business exposure, and so much more. You might say business and content strategy are my passion.

Years ago, when I first started working with new start-up businesses, I noticed there was a pattern with some of my clients. They would start out excited about a new adventure, and full of enthusiasm for their new business. Over time however, the reality of the day to day activities involved in running the business, slowly turned their excitement to disappointment or even frustration. Their dream of business ownership looked nothing like their new reality.

I started to look for answers. I had used the same process for all my clients, the same twelve learning modules, the same consulting practices. So, why did some of them build the business of their dreams, while others built a business they ultimately closed or sold because they didn't love it anymore? Why did the business not live up to their expectations?

The answer came to me the first time I took the StrengthsFinder test. I have always been a bit of an assessment geek. I love how they are so accurate and how much I learn about myself. I never pass up an opportunity to take another assessment.

This test was different, it focused on something new, my Strengths! Those things that I am naturally good at, so I gravitate toward them. It identified my strengths and told me what that might mean in a career or business. I loved this.

In contrast, the assessment also showed me things lower on my strengths scale. They don't call them weaknesses; they just fall lower on your scale of strengths. I was fascinated to see that they were things I didn't like to do and as a result, I often avoided.

Additionally, I learned the science behind the assessments shows we are happier and more fulfilled doing things we are good at, imagine that.

Could it be that those clients, who built a business they didn't love, had created a job for themselves that didn't consider their strengths? Did they build the RIGHT business for themselves, based on those things that would be fulfilling for them?

I knew I was onto something. If the science proves people are happier and more fulfilled when they are working in their strengths, I had to be sure my clients created a business around their strengths. So, armed with that new knowledge, I started having my new clients take the StrengthsFinder assessment when I first started coaching them.

To this day, new business clients start with a StrengthsFinder assessment. They find it valuable as they explore the options for their new business adventure, and I know how to best guide them toward a business that plays to their natural strengths. It has been transformational in my business; I am better able help my clients create a business they love.

If you have never done so, I encourage you to take the StrengthsFinder assessment as well. Our strengths and weaknesses make us who we are… learn to embrace them!

Self-Discovery

So, where do you start? You might have a very clear idea of what you want your new business to look like, or you may have NO idea what you want to do. Either way, let's start by talking about some self-discovery.

8 Ways to Mind Your Own Business

How well do you know yourself? Do you prefer to work collaboratively with a group, or do you prefer to work alone? Are you a creative person or an analytical one? The better you know yourself, the easier it will be to create a business that you love.

As you begin this journey, start with the desired end-result in mind. Before you start this new business, know what you want to do with your time. What activities do want to do, day in and day out? What tasks make you feel fulfilled and what things leaving you feeling drained or spent? Build your new business around those things you WANT to do, those tasks that you enjoy, they are probably your strengths.

Let's be honest, as a business owner you'll still have to do a few things you don't want to do, especially at first. In time, as resources allow, you'll be able to outsource them or hire someone to handle those tasks. The goal is to build a business out of the tasks that fill you up and bring satisfaction, I call that finding your passion.

Let me give you a good example from my own life. I have always known I loved to write. In fact, when I was eleven, I took some notebook paper and bound it together with some yarn to make a book. I was going to be an author and fill the world with my stories. When I was thirteen, I ghost wrote a children's book and I was hooked on the idea of being a writer and author.

What I didn't realize, of course, was that the life of an author is very solitary. It is countless hours at a keyboard, multiple manuscript revisions, and sending out query letters, trying to get a publisher to take your project. It is full of rejection. I had no way of knowing at such a young age, that the vision in my head was nothing like the reality of being an author.

I was sure I would be an author at some point but, as it sometimes does, life took me in a different direction. Probably because I am an extrovert and very social. I discovered a love for helping others succeed in business and have built a career around a consulting practice that does just that.

Yes, I am a published author and I continue to write, however, much of my time is spent helping my clients craft their message. Together we write their marketing content, their vision and mission statement, articles to gain them more exposure, and even their own book, to generate more leads for their business.

Can you see how those two paths look very different in the day to day tasks? I can't imagine being happy or fulfilled as just a writer and author. I love the personal connections I have with my clients. It's so satisfying when my clients have successes, and I am proud like a parent when we get their article or book published.

While it wasn't intentional, I created a business that is perfect for me, I truly love what I do. It happened the hard way, the long way around, over the years, as my business grew and changed. Save yourself some time and design it around your passions from the start. Be intentional.

As you consider the activities and tasks that you enjoy, those strengths that naturally make you happy or fulfilled, take plenty of notes. Pay close attention to Debbie in the next chapter, as she talks about staying true to yourself. Write down everything that comes to mind during your discovery, you might be surprised later by how they can fit together into a business you will love.

Due Diligence

Once you have defined what you think your new business should look like, it's time for some due diligence. Don't assume you know everything, do some research.

You will need to learn as much a possible about your new product or services. How it's being sold, where it's being sold, and how much people are paying for it. Google it (or whatever search engine you prefer) and write down everything you learn.

Weather you love it or hate it, the internet is an endless source of information. Of course, you can't believe everything you read, just because you found it on the web, but it is an incredible resource for data.

Research now to avoid mistakes that will cost you time and money later.

As you research your business idea, pay attention to how many others are already offering the same products or services. You've probably heard the saying, there is nothing new under the sun; just understand that your idea might not be unique, and that's okay.

All businesses need customers, who are willing and able to part with their money, for the goods and services they want or need. If you can't find anyone else offering those products or services, beware. Perhaps others have tried your idea, but no one was buying.

It is only a viable business if people are willing and able to pay for your products or services.

For example, if you want to make tutu's for sumo ballerinas, make sure there is a market for it.

Don't be discouraged if you find several businesses already doing what YOU want to do, in fact it proves there is a need for it in the marketplace. Find those who are doing it successfully and create a case study on each of them.

You want to know, what need they are filling. How they are different from their competitors. Who are their customers?

The more you can learn about their business model, the better. This is where you can really save yourself some grief later, no need to completely recreate the wheel!

After you've gathered the data during your due diligence, it's time to create your own strategic plan. This is the road map you will follow as you create your new business.

8 Ways to Mind Your Own Business

Strategic Plan

It can sound scary at first. A strategic plan is just a picture of what you want your business to look like, and how you want it to function. This is where you get it out of your head and onto paper, so you can get your thoughts and ideas organized. I like to call it brainstorming and blueprinting your business.

As you develop a plan, keep that end-result in mind, so you create a solid plan toward your ideal outcome. This will keep you from chasing after shiny objects that grab your attention along the way. Remember, if it doesn't move you toward your ideal outcome, don't include it.

Armed with a few case studies, look for ways your company might do it differently or perhaps better. In a sea of noise, you need a way to get noticed. What will make you stand out as unique? Remember to look back at your assessment results and incorporate your natural strengths where possible.

As you start your plan, it's a good time to assess where you're at personally. Not just your skills, but your assets as well. Starting a business will take money. It doesn't have to be a huge amount but realize you will need some resources. Don't quit your day job just yet.

Will you need a business loan to get started or will you bootstrap your new business, paying for things as you go? Are there classes you should take or certifications you could get, to help you succeed?

Be honest about where you are now and where you want to be when your business is successful.

It's worth mentioning that this process takes some time. In fact, my clients rarely do it in one sitting. It requires a lot of brain power and can even be exhausting. Take your time, get this part right. If you don't know where to start or you get stuck, find a strategist or coach to guide you.

It is easier to make a path correction before the concrete is poured!

A strategic plan is like a road map, showing you the most direct route to your desired destination. Once you understand where you are, and where you want to be, it's a simple matter of creating that written plan to get there. A map to follow. Chart out all the steps from start to finish and the end-result is your strategic plan!

While a written business plan is not always required for a new business, it is a helpful tool for any new business owner. If you will be getting funding for your new venture, you WILL need a business plan for the application process. Don't panic. Take your new strategic plan and create a business plan.

Your lender will be looking for some very specific information. They want to know you have done your due diligence and that your new business idea is sound. Include information about your closest competitors, what they charge, and how your business will be different. Don't forget to include financial projections and how you expect to pay yourself. There are free resources online for creating a basic business plan, but don't be afraid to check with your local business associations if you need help.

Decision Time

Now, you've decided you want to start a business and be your own boss. You are serious, or you wouldn't be spending your time with us, learning about mindset and strategies for the business start-up! So, how does this work? Let's recap.

First, spend some time in self-discovery, get clear about what you want to do with your time.

Then, do some due diligence about the products or services you want to offer, learning about the options and potential competition.

Next, put together a strategic plan to create, build, and launch your business. Use your strategic plan to create your business plan if you will need one.

Finally, make the decision already!

Weekly, I have a conversation with someone who has been planning to start their own business… sometimes for years. Usually, they just don't know where or how to start.

Sometimes it is uncertainty about HOW to get started, but often it is a fear of failure. They have so many questions, and no support system to cheer them on.

If this is you, I encourage you to find a business coach or consultant. If you have the resources to hire a coach, it can be some of the best money you will ever spend on your new business. Again, due diligence is important here. Check references!

You don't have to do it alone. We all need support and encouragement, all of us! Find a few social media groups to participate in, a local networking group to join, and a mentor who has already forged a path in the direction you want to go.

It's time to get started, are you ready to take the leap into business ownership and change your future? If you are, mark this day on your calendar, and get started.

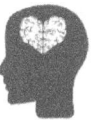

Inspired Passion

Setting sail on a new adventure is both an exciting and potentially scary process. It is like a ship taking off for an unknown destination, and we have no idea how long the journey will take to get there, nor if we will ever reach the shore full of hope and promise. All we know is we are willing to take that leap of faith... that first step into the unknown.

If you are at this stage of your journey, I can tell you, I know exactly how you feel. For many years I worked for corporate organisations, slowly becoming more and more institutionalised, more disillusioned, and increasingly fearful of losing my job. Yet in my heart there was nothing I wanted more than to run my own business. Making this adventure would mean stepping away from so many years of training and experience. It would mean taking a deep look at myself and rediscovering ME and what I wanted out of life. It would mean taking a voyage away from fear and turning it into a knowingness that every step was inspired by my passion.

I literally felt my fear and did it anyway. And so much of that journey was in my mind. I learnt to step away from fear. I learnt to trust me. To trust that the universe and life would support me. I had to get back in touch with my intuition again, for I had been ignoring it for a number of years, and taking this journey meant I needed to hear it more than ever. Overall, I learnt to reconnect with me, and be open and receptive to new ways of doing things and new ways of being.

It has been a journey which has tested my courage, but it has been so worthwhile. I have grown so much as a person, and I know you will too. For if I can do it, you can do it too.

It all starts with being clear on what you want. For me, becoming a Life & Leadership Coach was like coming home. I had literally come full circle in my life, resorting back to what I was interested in when I was 18 or 19. Yet in my career, I had gone from being an Administrator, to a Laboratory Clerk, to an actress, to a Chartered Management Accountant, to a Business Analyst, and then when I finally became a coach, it felt like coming home.

So, how do you feel about stepping out on your entrepreneurial journey? Do you know where you are headed? Maybe you are taking Clara's suggestion and using StrengthFinders. Or maybe you are sitting quietly and getting in touch with that inner wisdom within, which always knows the right answer for you, like I did through meditation and journaling. No matter how you have come to your decision, to step out on the great entrepreneurial journey, notice whether you have supporters waving you off. Or whether you have some people saying, 'what on earth are you giving all that up for?' like I did.

When you hold your vision of the future cupped in your hand like a precious seedling, and you nurture it with supportive inner dialogue and inspiring actions, you will find it doesn't matter whether you have supporters or nay-sayers. You will know in your heart that you are doing the right thing.

The problem is we don't always have supportive inner dialogue to help us along the way. We listen to other people and we doubt ourselves. We may have all sorts of beliefs about what we can and cannot do, which we have learnt over the years since early childhood. These beliefs can unknowingly get in our way and sabotage our success. So, during our journey together, I will share with you how I became more consciously aware of my own beliefs and how I changed them to support my new life and business intentions.

With any journey it is always best to not only know the destination, but to also know where you are starting from. Like with any GPS system, in order to plan your route, it needs to know where you are now. So, this is where we will start.

Where are you now, and what do you believe?

The first step to really getting to know where you are right now, and to understand your motivations behind your actions, thoughts and behaviours, is to jot them down daily in a journal.

This is a great way to become more consciously aware of how life plays out on the outside and correspondingly on the inside. Our life is a mirror, and when we have drama on the outside, it is usually a signifier that there is drama going on within.

Most of the time we go through life without realising the patterns which are playing out in life. Journaling is a great way to become consciously aware of that. I would suggest that every day you write a few pages about your day. Not just what happened, but how you felt, what you learnt (particularly about yourself), and pose any questions you want to know the answers to.

This may seem a bit strange if you've never done it before, but I have found it such an eye-opening experience, that I still do it almost every day. We will explore using journals and how this can help build our business more in the coming chapters.

Right now, though, it is really helpful to start understanding your beliefs and how they play out in your life. You are so used to your beliefs that you hardly realise they are having an effect on your life. Yet they will affect the decisions you make, the level of success you accept into your life, as well as the relationships you have with others.

In the same way a computer has an operating system, your beliefs are like your operating system and they affect everything you do and how you do it.

8 Ways to Mind Your Own Business

Whether you realise it or not, a lot of your beliefs were formed during your early childhood. At that stage of your life, you heard others tell you what you were good at, what you couldn't do, what your boundaries were. You didn't question whether what they said was right or wrong. You just accepted them as your own and allowed them to form how your life would continue.

So, if you are able, I would like you to write down the answers to these questions. If you can't write them down now, let the questions mull in your mind and journal on them later.

1. What are your beliefs about success?

I would like you to write or think of as many things as you can about success. Like how you measure success? What does success look like for you? What does success feel like for you? Do you feel successful now? What were you taught about success when you were growing up? There really is no right or wrong answers. There are only things to learn about yourself and that is OK.

2. What are your beliefs about failure?

Again, think about what failure means to you. What does it look like? What does it feel like? What did you learn about failure from your family and wider community when you were growing up? And what have you learnt about it as an adult? Write as many things as you can think of. Remember there are no right or wrong answers. All is good.

3. What are your beliefs about work?

What does work look like for you? What did you believe about work when you were growing up? Do you think work should be hard or easy? What did you learn about work, from your family or from your school? Do you think you should get well paid for doing the work you love? Again write, or think, of as many things as you can before moving on to the next question. The more things you can think of, the more understanding you will have of your beliefs and how they may be supporting or getting in the way of your success and happiness.

4. What do you think about financial prosperity?

Talking about money is always an interesting subject. It can bring up so many emotions. So how do you feel about money? Do you think money must be hard earned, or do you think it comes easily? How much money do you think you deserve? Is it more or less than the money you create now? What did you learn about money from your family? Do you always have money, or does it seem to slip through your fingers?

5. What do you believe you deserve?

This is a really big question, so let's break it down. How much do you think you deserve for your new business to pay you? Do you think you deserve for your business to pay you straight from the beginning? Do you think you will start deserving payment from your business after three, or six months? Or longer? Do you deserve to get paid first? Or are you last on the list of getting? How much success do you think you deserve? What did you learn about deserving from your family as you were growing up?

6. And finally, what do think about fulfilment?

What does feeling fulfilled mean to you? Do you expect to experience it in your leisure time, or your work time? How do you experience fulfilment? What did you learn about living a fulfilled life from your family and wider community when you were growing up? Is your life fulfilled now? Do you deserve it to be fulfilled? Moving forward, how does a fulfilled life look and feel to you?

These are wonderful questions to ask yourself, for they help you to start thinking about who you are, what you believe and what you want moving forward. If some of these questions got you thinking about how your beliefs may not be supporting your new journey, don't worry.

This book is a journey of building your new business, as well as building a new supportive attitude. You really do have a choice, and you will learn how you can choose the thinking which supports you moving forward. What are your intentions moving forward?

Intentions are like goals. I avoid using the word goal because it can work for some people and empower their journey forwards, yet for other people it can leave them feeling pressurised and restricted. It can also cause us to have such a strong focus on one particular thing, that we miss even better opportunities because they just pass us by, and we don't even see them.

I think the biggest reason why I don't use the word goals is because it generally focuses our attention on the external things we want, like the job, the money, the car, the partner, the house, or the business. But that leaves out the internal goals, like how you want to BE as a person.

So, just for a moment, I'd like you to imagine you are a beautiful old oak tree. Your branches are all immaculately shaped and your leaves are all polished and clean. These branches represent how the world sees you. They are the things you own, as well as your actions and behaviours.

Now think about the roots of the tree. They are the tree's life force. They keep it anchored to the ground and absorb a supply of nutrients to help it grow. The tree needs deep, well-spaced, healthy, anchored roots in order to survive. Just like the tree, we too need strong roots, and our roots are our emotional intelligence, our emotional resilience, and our self-esteem.

If you focus on all the external things you want, but forget about strengthening your roots, then just like a tree with shallow roots can come crashing down amidst a storm, you too could feel the emotional effects of not having a strong and resilient inner world, the next time you face one of life's big challenges.

So, as you step out on your journey of building your business, I would encourage you to do so with two types of intentions. The intentions you want to DO (which includes what you want to have), and the intention of how you want to BE.

In your mind, or on paper if you are able to, put the heading, My Intentions to DO. Underneath I would like you to create a list of things you want to do. Think of them in as much detail as possible. It is also useful if you put a reason why next to each intention, as well as giving them a date by which you intend to realise them. If you haven't got a notebook and pen to hand, don't worry. Allow your mind to come up with the things you want and trust that you will remember them later so you can write them down. It is a really good idea to write them down when you can, as an intention in your head is strong but an intention externalised is even stronger.

It really doesn't matter whether your intentions are small or really big. The idea at this stage is to allow yourself to dream. Don't worry about whether you believe you can achieve them or not. Or what other people will say about your intentions. Just create a list, five or six things is a really great start. Think of all areas of your life too. Starting and growing a business is great, but if that overtakes your life, to the detriment of all else, then you won't necessarily find it fulfilling in the longer term.

For true balance in life you want to consider health, relationships (both personal and professional), financial prosperity, and work. When you think of building your intentions to support ALL areas of your life, you are more likely to create a life which feels successful and meaningful to you.

Now that you have your list of things you want to DO; I would like you to create a list of things you want to BE. Where your list of things to DO are like the branches of the oak tree, your list of things to BE, are like the roots.

So how do you want to be? Do you want to be happy? I've never encountered anyone who doesn't. Do you want to be courageous, loving, forgiving of yourself and others, self-assured, confident, assertive, and have a fabulously loving and nourishing inner dialogue supporting a high self-esteem? You could also think about the way you want to handle difficult situations or challenges. Maybe you want to feel resourceful, knowing you can handle any situation. You may want to be calm and not knee jerk to challenges. You may want to have access to inner peace, no matter what is going on around you. The choice really is yours.

Again, write down or make a mental note, of a list of around five or six things and entitle it My Intentions to BE list. If you can't write them down now, remember to jot them down later.

So now you have two wonderful lists. A, My Intentions to DO list for all the things you want to create, achieve, and acquire. And My Intentions to BE list, for how you want to think and feel.

This is such a wonderful way to start your journey. Being true and honest about what change you want to create in your life, is a fabulous first step to creating it.

Are your intentions really yours?

8 Ways to Mind Your Own Business

Before we move any further, I'd like to invite you to re-look at your lists. Really go through them and think about why you put those things on your list. You may think, *because I want them.* Yet it is interesting how often we list intentions which aren't really and truly our own.

As you think of each item on your lists, pay real attention to why you want them. Is it because the doing of it fills your heart with joy? Does it feel like you are following your bliss? Or is there another reason?

We have all done things, for one reason or another, that don't make our heart sing. Perhaps we felt like we had to, or we did it to please someone else.

If this is you, maybe you feel at a deep level that by achieving these intentions you will make the other person happy, then their approval will make you happy. Sometimes we get so caught up in fulfilling someone else's dreams that we don't fulfil our own. We think if we make them happy, then they will show us their approval, which will make us happy.

The problem when we do this, is that our happiness rests on another person. What happens if they don't approve? Or, no matter what we do, we don't meet their expectations. Then we won't be happy.

Without realising it we are giving away our power. We are placing our happiness in someone else's hands. So that puts us at the mercy of another person. If this is you, then I would urge you to relook at your intentions. If you do something to please someone else, but it doesn't please you, you could eventually become resentful and unhappy. The best course of action is to do what makes you happy.

I am telling you this from experience. Years ago, I took the wrong career path in becoming an accountant. I did it for two reasons. Firstly, to prove to others that I could do it, which you know isn't the best reason to do something. The other reason was, my employer offered to enroll me at college one day a week, as well as paying for all the training costs involved in qualifying as a Chartered Management Accountant.

My intellect told me I would be nuts to turn down an offer down like that. I told myself it was a good idea to spend six years of my life deep in study, when my heart was telling me the opposite. But I didn't listen to my heart. My head, I thought, knew better. Even five years into my study, my intuition was still asking me, what are you doing this for? But I ignored it. I thought intellectually I knew best. But I didn't. Over time my heart proved it had known all along that accountancy wasn't the best option for me. If only I had listened to it earlier.

So, now as you look and think about your lists, ask yourself whether they leave you feeling excited, expectant, or maybe a little nervous? The main thing is to make sure that you really are following your inspired passions, which should be in alignment with your strengths as explained by Clara in the last chapter. If your intentions aren't exciting you, it may be worth spending a little more time on exploring your real intentions. Know ALL is possible.

The last thing I want you to know before we end this chapter, is that everything you have on your Intention lists is possible. There is everything to gain from taking that leap of faith into the unknown and following your inspired passion. In following your passion, your intuition, your bliss or whatever else you want to call it, you will only ever be led in the right direction for you.

At this stage things may feel exciting and just a little bit scary, but I want you to know that you are only ever attracted to the things which you can create. You have everything within you to create your life, just the way you want it. You may not fully believe this right now, but as you work through the Inspired sections of this book, your belief in your ideas and yourself, will grow at the same time as your business grows.

Just know that all is possible.

8 Ways to Mind Your Own Business

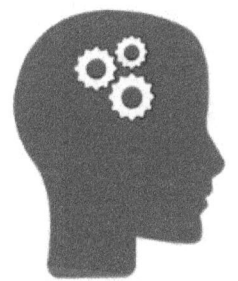 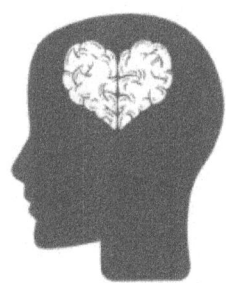

2nd Way

Creation MATTERS

The start-up stages of any new business... is my favorite part. Perhaps that's why I have spent so much of my career, helping clients start a new business.

Making the decision to get started can sometime be scary, but you are here because you have crossed that bridge. Now the fun of creation begins.

Creation can be fun and exhilarating, but also challenging and intimidating, especially if you don't consider yourself a creative person. Take a deep breath, I promise this is not difficult. We will guide you through the basics.

With your strategic plan in front of you, it's time to create the pieces of your business. Decisions need to be made about the company name, brand colors, and focus. During your discovery and strategic planning, some of these decisions might have been made already. If not, take some time to get clear on these items before moving on.

If you find yourself struggling with this, you might want to find someone to brainstorm your ideas with or even a coach or mentor.

Great Name

It's time to pick a great name for your new company. Picking a company name can be a challenge, it's often a sticking point for start-up companies. Your name is usually the first thing your potential customer will see, so choose it carefully. There are a few things to keep in mind when making this decision.

The name should make it clear what your business has to offer. A tagline can be used to clarify what products or services you offer. It can be tempting to use a name that has meaning to you personally, but be careful, you want the potential customer to easily recognize what you have to offer them. The exception to this rule is for those building a personal brand, they are creating an entire brand around their own name. If that is you, that work is done!

Also, avoid making up words that no one will recognize or spelling them differently, just so you can be unique. This usually tends to confuse potential customers and make your name less memorable.

A pun or play on words can be fun, but I caution you again, it could backfire. As a writer, I tend to enjoy wordplay. So, a few years ago, I started using the term WordCrafter, to describe myself to clients who wanted to write a book. After all, I help people craft their words into a message… I thought it was brilliant!

8 Ways to Mind Your Own Business

Unfortunately, most people didn't connect with the term I had created. Now I wasn't naming a business, so it was easy to correct this mistake, once I discovered it wasn't resonating with my potential clients.

It's human nature to avoid using words that we aren't sure how to say or spell, so don't alienate those who might be timid about trying to pronounce an unusual name. Remember the KISS method, *Keep It Super Simple*, whenever possible. You might remember the KISS method as Keep It Simple Stupid, but I find it unnecessarily harsh.

If you're still stuck on the name, I recommend a great book by Alexandra Watkins - Hello, My Name is Awesome. She offers a ton of helpful tips for picking a great name.

Perfect Logo

With the name decided on, a logo is the next step in the process. Your logo is a visual representation of your business. Its sole purpose is for brand recognition. Take some time to consider what you want your logo to say about your company.

It can have a cartoon quality or feel more like a Rembrandt, so long as it remains simple and versatile. You will want to use it in multiple places for branding and marketing, it's helpful to have a part you can pull out to stand alone. That piece works well for a social media avatar.

Think about Target, or Nike, they can drop the names from their logo and we still know who they are. I'm not saying you need to act like one of the big dogs, they are branding at a very high level, but some simple choices now can make branding easier.

Right Colors

Now, this might surprise you a bit, but colors really matter. You've probably seen comments or articles about the meaning of different colors.

In truth, the colors themselves don't have meaning. There is a psychology around colors, it's about the symbolism we have culturally assigned to them. That might sound like a lot of woo woo, but how a color makes our potential customer feel... should matter to us.

When deciding on your company colors, it can be helpful to find a picture that represents your business well, take note of the colors. Or find a color chart online and make an educated choice about your brand colors.

Laser Focus

During your strategic planning you learned about yourself and what made you feel fulfilled. You might have already considered who you want to serve, but often new business owners feel like everyone is their potential customer.

8 Ways to Mind Your Own Business

While it might be true that anyone COULD be your customer, it is very difficult to cut through the marketing noise when you are talking to everyone. Get laser focused on who you really want to serve, and who you best serve. Not everyone is your ideal customer, that perfect fit for you and your business.

This doesn't mean you won't serve others, who are not your ideal customer, you will still attract some of them. It does mean your marketing message will be very clear and will attract more of your ideal customers. Who doesn't want that?

It feels counterintuitive but being laser focused is the secret to business growth. Your business will be stronger if you stick to the core of your offerings, rather than diversifying too much.

Company Culture

Now that some of the basics are decided, let's talk about the culture you want to create in your new company. You might wonder what that even means. Well, it's a bit like a personality for your company.

The culture in a company can seem intangible, it's hard to put your finger on it but you can definitely FEEL culture. Your customers and employees will feel it, and it will be a driving force in your business. You can be purposeful and create a culture, or let one develop on its own… although you might not be happy with those results. I prefer to be intentional.

The work environment, as well as the company values, mission, vision, and goals, will work together to create your company culture. While the environment and company goals should be continually evolving; the company values, mission, and vision, are foundational pieces you must intentionally create.

Company core values are usually driven by the personal values of the business owner or founder. Take just a few minutes to recognize what those are for you. As you articulate them, it is easy to create a written values statement for your new business. These values will be the guiding principles in everything your business does. Integrity, commitment, accountability, and fun; are examples of core values you might want in your new business.

Based on your new company values, now you can create your company vision and mission statements.

The vision statement is simply a declaration of your vision for the future of your company. It is usually a one sentence statement about your company aspirations. You will want to share it with customers and employees alike, so everyone knows where the company is headed.

For example, here is my company vision statement for Intentional Influence. To provide a strategic and intentional method for SAVVY Influencers to craft their message and share it with the world.

8 Ways to Mind Your Own Business

While the vision statement looks to the future, the mission statement is about the day to day activities. It is the mission at hand, or what you do in order to achieve the long-term vision of the company.

For example, here is my company mission statement. Intentional Influence was created to provide resources and tools to help new, but SAVVY influencers, build their influence. We help them craft their message, write their book, create their signature speech, and strategically lead for greater influence.

Since this is another sticking point for many companies, it might be helpful to find someone to facilitate this process.

I once worked with a well-established company that was plagued with internal issues. They constantly chased after the next shiny object related to their industry, and while they were able to remain profitable, the resulting turmoil, took its toll on everyone in the company.

After some discovery and analysis of their business, I discovered they had no clear values and no written vision or mission statement. Any time a new opportunity came along, they would head in a new direction. They had nothing foundational to look at when making decisions for the company.

It sounds so simple, but once they created these pieces of their business, things changed for the better. When a new opportunity came along, they could see if it was a good fit with their values. They would quickly know if it would move them toward their vision of the future, and if it fit with their current day to day mission. They then had better tools, for better decisions about the direction of the company.

This is just a cautionary tale, create these foundational pieces for your culture now, or later you will be looking to hire someone to help you fix issues later.

Setting Goals

Setting goals for your company is about creating a measuring tool for your progress. You need a way to measure where you are, compared to where you want to be.

My husband and I both own a business. At our house, we revisit our goals and vision board twice a year, for our businesses and for us personally.

At the end of the year, we assess what we accomplished during the year and where we want to go in the coming year. Then during the summer… we measure, monitor, and adjust our actions and goals to keep us on track.

Since goals are a moving target and always changing, let's talk about the basics of goal setting.

You've probably heard the concept of creating SMART goals, but I like to use my own version of the idea.

8 Ways to Mind Your Own Business

I call them SAVVY goals...

- Strategic
- Actionable
- Values Based
- Visionary
- You Focused

As you create your goals, pay attention, and see if they are SAVVY goals.

I am a strategic person by nature. Planning gives me a sense of order and control over my own direction. Of course, intellectually I realize that control is an illusion, but I still find comfort in the details that come from planning. You might not find the same comfort in planning but TRUST me, the value of a sound strategy goes far beyond feelings.

Your company goals will give you guidance and direction, but new goals will emerge as your business grows. Sometimes goals change, and that's okay. They are just goals, not written in blood or set in stone, feel free to change or modify them as you or your business changes. Debbie will talk more about how to do this effectively in the Inspired chapters.

If you know me personally or follow me online, you have seen my Word of the Year posted each January. This word of the year is created as a by-product of what I want to achieve, my goals for the coming year. Sometimes it is large and vague, other times it seems very focused, but either way, it is intended to move me in a specific direction for the new calendar year.

Feel free to create and express your goals in a way that is comfortable for you.

Just as they are for me, your goals become a part of the strategy you will use to create and grow your new business. Take a minute to review your goals then pick a word or theme for the year; it is a great tool for decision making, as you shape your company culture.

Inspired Creation

Now you have a powerful set of SAVVY goals, or as I like to call them intentions, that will move you forward.

I call them intentions because the word goal works for some people but has a demotivating effect on others. It can also reduce flexibility in our thinking and so create tunnel vision. The word intention is softer and allows for an expansion of thinking. Since you only intend to do this thing, it is not set in stone, so it can be changed as circumstances around change.

Having intentions for things you want to achieve, is such a wonderful position to be. Without these intentions you may've chosen to stand still, to not move forward. Or you may've done what you thought you should do and ended up at the wrong destination. Everything in life is a choice.

We can choose to procrastinate, to not believe in ourselves, to blame and become a victim. We choose to stay stuck, go in the wrong direction, or we choose to move forward and create the life and business we want.

Right now, you are doing the most powerful of these, to create from a place of inspiration. This is distinct and different then creating from a place of intellect, where there is the potential of creating for the wrong reasons. Remember how I pursued the wrong career in accountancy because intellectually I thought it was a good idea. When we try to create from a place of intellect and not from inspiration then we can end up making the wrong turn.

Now that you are inspired to create the life and business you want; I would like to ask you to do an exercise with me. As you do so, allow your imagination to follow along and see where it takes you.

Protecting your Seedling of Creation

A seed is a wonderful powerhouse of creation. Within it contains everything needed for that seed to grow into a strong tree or plant. All it needs is the right environment in which to be planted, and the power of creation takes over. If you were to cut the seed open you wouldn't see an image of what the seed will become inside of it, all you see are the inner elements of the seed. What you do see, though, is potential for growth.

Your intentions are like seeds. They all have the potential for growth and to bloom into realisations. What they need is the right environment in order to flourish.

So just for a moment I would like to you imagine that you have your hands cupped out in front of you. Within your cupped hands lies some nutritious soil in which you've planted one of your seeds of intentions.

Your intention is precious, so you look after this seed. You allow the rain to water it and the sun to warm it. You create the right environment for life to begin. Slowly and surely the seedling starts to germinate. As the seedling pops its head above the level of the soil it unfurls and looks towards its nourishing and supportive environment to help it to grow.

Still cupped in your hands, this seedling requires your care and attention. If a weed pops its head about the surface, you are best to pull it out. For your seedling needs room to grow. If weeds are left to root and take hold, soon your seedling will be surrounded by weeds and it will struggle for life. If left unattended, eventually the weeds will crowd the seedling and it will die.

Now think back to your intentions. In order for them to flourish, you need to provide them with the environment in which to flourish. Then as they grow you nurture them, so they manifest into their fullest possibilities.

In the same way that weeds can stifle the seedling, our thinking can stifle our intentions. Every time we worry about achieving them, feel doubt about their creation, or listen to a nay-sayer, it is like a weed popping up and threatening to cut off our seedling from its life supply.

The words you say, and the words you think are powerful. They are more than mere words. They are the energetic force which inspires creation. So, I'd like to invite you to get a deeper understanding of the words you use.

How You Think

The problem with our thinking is we are so used to it, that it feels natural and normal. We can easily believe that everyone else thinks the same way as we do. Yet they don't. Our thinking is habitual and personal to us. On average we have around 60,000 to 80,000 thoughts per day. And the vast percentage of those are the same as we thought yesterday, and the day before.

Since our thinking feels so natural, we can become consciously unaware of how they play out in our life. So, I would like to run through an exercise with you to help give you greater clarity on how you think.

Once you have read the following, I'd like you to run through the exercise with your eyes closed as this will enhance the experience of the exercise. Otherwise just follow along in your imagination.

To start with, I would like you to relax and to take your awareness off whatever is going on in your mind and to place it on your breath. You can concentrate on the rise and fall of your belly, or the feeling of the air as it comes in and out of your nostrils. Take your time and allow each out-breath to relax you a little more.

8 Ways to Mind Your Own Business

Now in your mind I would like you to see yourself waking up on a normal everyday morning. As you awake to the day, pay attention to the first thoughts that pop into your head. And pay attention to how you feel. Are you pleased to welcome in a new day? Or are you unhappy that your alarm has woken you too early?

Then see yourself getting up and going about your morning routine. How do you feel as you step into the shower? What are your thoughts when you catch sight of yourself in the mirror? Is it a leisurely routine, or are you in a hurry?

Imagine moving into the next part of your day. Maybe that is a commute into work. As you sit in the car, bus, or train, notice how you feel and what your thoughts are. Are they different depending on the level of traffic? What about if you get stuck in a traffic jam? And what about if it makes you late?

Then in your mind allow the next part of your day to unfold. See yourself doing what you normally do during the morning. Maybe you are on your own. Maybe you are with other people. As you allow your mind movie to continue, pay attention to your thoughts and feelings, and how these might change depending on who you are with and what you are doing.

In your mind your day reaches lunch time. What do you do with this segment of your day? What do you choose to eat? Who do you spend your time with? Do you rush through your food whilst sat at a desk, hardly paying attention to what you eat? Or are you giving yourself some time to recuperate before moving into the afternoon?

As your day moves into the afternoon, how do you think and feel about this part of your day? What is happening? Who are you with? Allow the movie in your mind to play out this segment of your day and make mental notes of your thoughts and feelings.

With the afternoon turning into early evening, maybe you are making your commute home. If you are, how do you feel and what are your thoughts about this part of your day? Are you glad to be leaving the office? Or are you feeling joyful about seeing friends or family soon. Do these thoughts and feelings change if the traffic is heavy?

As the rest of your evening plays out in your mind. Continue to pay attention to what you are doing, who you are with, and what you think and feel about this part of your day.

Now I want you to move this day right to the very end, when you are in bed and about to go to sleep. Pay attention to your last thoughts and feelings of the day. Has it been a good day? Or are you glad it is over?

If you have had your eyes closed during this, you can stretch and open your eyes now. If you have your journal handy, jot down all the things that came to you. In particular your thoughts and your feelings. If you can't write them down just now, mull over them in your mind and write them down later.

8 Ways to Mind Your Own Business

This may be the first time you've become consciously aware of your thinking. Sometimes this can be a real eye opener. As I said, our thoughts can be so habitual that we don't really realise how we talk to ourselves. But now you may have a better idea and that is an empowering place to be.

You see thoughts aren't just thoughts... they are mini creators. Words have power and they can help you along your journey to creating your intentions, or they get in your way.

The Push Me-Pull You of Creation

Do you remember the Doctor Dolittle film? In the original version was a Push Me-Pull You. It was a two headed creature rather like a llama. At one end of its body was a head looking straight ahead, and the other end of its body it had another head pointing in the opposite direction.

How confusing would that be! You wouldn't know whether you are coming or going?

So, when one part of the Push Me-Pull You thinks it's moving forwards, the other half feels it is moving backwards, and vice versa. You can imagine that it would be really easy to get stuck and not know which direction to move.

If we go back to thinking about the power of our words, they are a little bit like the Push Me-Pull You. They will either take us in the direction of what we want, or away from it.

So, recall the thoughts and feelings you had when you envisioned your normal day, and think about the ebb and flow of your thoughts and feelings. Did some parts of your day feel good and others not so good? Did the whole day feel wonderful? Or did you just want to get through the day as quickly as you could, so you could start afresh tomorrow? Did you find that you criticised yourself? Maybe you berated yourself for doing something silly. Maybe you judged yourself for the way you look. Or maybe you judged the actions of another person.

Know that whatever you were thinking, is what it is… there is no right or wrong. There is just awareness and some learning to do.

If you found it difficult to capture your thinking whilst doing the exercise, focus your attention on how you felt. Feelings are your barometer. If you feel good, then great, you must be thinking good thoughts. You can't have good thoughts and feel bad, it just doesn't work that way. On the other hand, if your feelings weren't so good, know this is the time to lovingly pay attention to your thoughts.

The Language of Constraint

You may be wondering how all this ties together? How does the seedling of my intentions and my thinking during the day fit in with a Push Me-Pull You? Well I'll explain.

Your intention is something you want to manifest. As we said earlier, you want to make sure that the weeds of doubt, worry, anxiety, and any negative thoughts from others, are removed. Otherwise they stifle the growth of your intention.

So, like the Push Me-Pull You which moves forwards and backwards, your thoughts do too. They can push you in the direction of achieving your intentions or move you away from it. So, without realising it you could be self-sabotaging your success.

Words like, I can do it, everything is unfolding perfectly, and, I know everything will fall into place, move you in the direction of achieving your intentions. They are positive, life supportive, and make you feel good.

On the other hand when you think, I'm never going to be able to do this, I'm not good enough, I never get things right, or, what makes me think I can build a successful business, these move you away from what you want. The negative thinking is literally pulling you in the wrong direction!

So, think back to when you visualised your normal day. Re-read what you wrote in your journal about your experience of that exercise. Pay attention to the language you used and the feelings you experienced. All the good stuff you thought and felt was moving you towards the creation of your intention. Likewise, all the negative thinking, doubts, worries, fear, anxiety, basically anything that didn't feel good, was moving you away from what you wanted.

This is how we self-sabotage ourselves. We allow our thinking to get in our own way! And as I've said before, it's so habitual we don't even realise we are doing it most of the time.

Now that you are starting to gain an awareness there are three key practices to start doing

1. Keep your list of intentions to yourself until they are strong enough to share. Your initial intentions are like young seedlings and are fragile and need protecting. When you are first establishing your belief in achieving a new desire, someone else's negative opinion of either your idea, or your ability to carry it out can easily squash your dreams. They are the weeds that will crowd around your intention and stifle it if you aren't careful. A new intention is fragile, and it doesn't take a lot to destroy it. So only share your intentions once it is fully established in your thinking.

2. Become more self-aware of the language you use. When you catch yourself criticising, judging, berating, doubting, or worrying, then lovingly change your thinking to something that is more life supportive. Turn the negative thoughts around into positive affirmations. Instead of saying, I'll never be able to do that! Say instead, I have all the resources within me to handle any situation. Know this to be true for you. If that seems too far out of reach and unbelievable, soften it by saying, I am willing to have all the resources within me to handle any situation.

3. Release the need to attach a deadline date to every intention. Although this may help motivate

some people, it can also hinder the creation process. For our sub-conscious mind will work to that deadline, potentially slowing up the process which would have otherwise happened quicker. When you daily do the work in this chapter, you will find that inspiration will strike. As it does take action on it immediately. For you are being nudged gently into the right direction at the right time. The universe has a better idea of ideal timing than we do, so go with it.

Crossing the Bridge

Keeping the faith and cultivating that inner knowingness that your intentions will work out are things which may require constant work. I think of it like this... I am standing on one side of the riverbank knowing that what I want isn't here, it is on the other riverbank. And my thinking can go in one of two directions.

I can either feel the lack of not having it. What I want isn't here and that makes me unhappy. That can leave me feeling disheartened, and the more I focus on what I want and how not having it makes me feel, the unhappier I get. My thinking can quickly spiral downwards, and before I know it my thinking has spiralled so far down, I can no longer see any point in carrying on! That is the way our thinking can go, if we let it.

Or, as I stand and look across the river and see on the other riverbank all the things I want to have in my life and business, I can know they are waiting for me. They are letting me know that they are there. They may be out of reach, but they are a possibility. That can feel good if I can see a way of getting across the river.

Whatever your perspective, what you have are two riverbanks with a fast-flowing river in between, and a question of how to get from one side to the other.

Now comes the magic bit, and I want you to be open and receptive to hearing these really important next steps.

Firstly, making conscious use of positive and supportive thinking is like constructing a bridge. And secondly, you can use your imagination to walk across the bridge and experience everything you want as if it is already here.

Your thinking is your support mechanism. Every time you think, or say, something which affirms what you want and raises your belief in achieving it, it is like laying a girder of the bridge down. Before long, each thing you think and say is layering down lots of girders and a bridge has been formed. Along with a deep knowingness that what you want is going to be yours.

Secondly, you use your imagination to walk across the bridge. In doing this you literally span the space from where we are now, to where you want to be. Your imagination is the link building on your words.

Our imagination is an under-rated, yet amazingly powerful tool. We use it all the time, mostly unconsciously and usually to create some disastrous mind movie! Or was that just me?

I can remember a time when my mind was amazing at making up scary stories. How things would be if I lost my job. Or if my daughter went missing. Or my dog was hit by a car. On and on the endless stream of bad things would go on in my head. The more free-reign I gave them, the more license they had to create even more elaborate versions of disasters! I smile now when I think back to how I let my mind rule me.

As soon as I started to use my mind in constructive ways things began to change. In my mind I started to cross the bridge from where I was to where I wanted to be. Then I was creating mind movies which felt good. They were full of the things I wanted to do, and of the business I wanted to run. I paid no attention to how these things would happen. I just enjoyed the experience of playing them out in my mind as if they had already happened.

Doing this took me back to my childhood. When I was around nine or ten, I loved solving puzzles. Puzzles like the Rubik's cube, or puzzles in books. It didn't matter. There were times when I couldn't solve them no matter how hard I tried. So, I would ask the universe to provide me with the answer. I would then release the need to know now, and trust that a solution would be given. More often than not, during the night my dream would show me how to solve it, or at least do the next part of the puzzle. It was amazing.

Because I was letting go of my need to work out how to do it, it allowed my subconscious to reveal to me what I needed to do. Now I am not suggesting that you use your dreams to solve problems, although they can help. What I am suggesting is that you get past knowing how to span the bridge, and just allow it to happen in your imagination.

As an adult I forgot this wonderful skill and it was many years before I re-discovered it. You don't need to believe me when I say that it works. Just try it for yourself and see. It really does reduce your level of doubts, fears, and worries, and in turn your inner dialogue becomes more supportive. Over time you will get that deep inner knowingness that what you want is really possible.

Commit yourself to practicing this. Weave it into your everyday life. It really is just like daydreaming… and you can do this anywhere. You could be waiting for a bus, be stuck in traffic, walking the dog, cooking a meal. Anywhere. Have fun with it.

In addition to this, practice using supportive language. Always be gentle with yourself. If you catch yourself using negative self-talk, lovingly bring yourself back into alignment. Berating yourself never works.

Know that this is a process, it's not a destination. Using positive self-talk along with your imagination can help you to create your future the way you want it. As your levels of belief and inner knowingness rise, so will your understanding that you deserve all good in your life. That you can build the business you want.

You may think that this is all very well and good, but I can't build a business in my head. Just have faith in this process and we will explore more in future chapters. All you need to know is that this works and that it leads to you taking inspired action. It is this inspired action which makes all the difference.

8 Ways to Mind Your Own Business

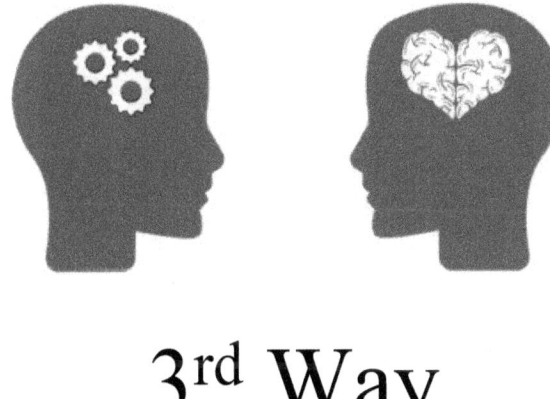

3rd Way

8 Ways to Mind Your Own Business

Business MATTERS

So far, we have talked about the pieces of your business that your customers or clients will see and feel from your business. The passion you bring to your work, the benefits they will receive from your products or services, the culture of your business, and the visual branding you have created.

All the planning, strategy, and creativity is my favorite part of a new start-up. These things may have taken some time to get done, but you should be feeling good about the progress you've made on your new business. Now we need to focus on some really important business basics.

First, let me say, I am not a lawyer or tax professional. My intent here is to give you an understanding of the basics for business. It is always prudent to seek the advice of a professional for clarification as you start this new business.

Depending on the country you live in, business might be governed by the Provinces, Departments, or Territories the business resides in. My business experience and knowledge has been gained in the United States, and I am NOT knowledgeable about other countries, so be sure to check with your local administrative officials for guidance on the paperwork and requirements.

In the Unites States, we have a system that is used nationwide, it keeps everything consistent. It is governed at the state level and regulated by the Internal Revenue Service. As a business owner you get to choose if you want to do business as a sole proprietor, a corporation, or a partnership. After talking to the appropriate professionals, you must decide what makes sense for you. Let's explore some options.

Sole Proprietor

A sole proprietor is usually just one person, you. You'd be doing business under your own social security number for tax purposes, and all your liabilities, are your own at a personal level. If you plan to be a very small company, without employees or large debts, this might work for you. Keep in mind, you will have no corporate protection as a sole proprietor, so if you get sued for some reason, it's all you baby.

When I was eighteen, I started my first business when I became an Avon Lady. It was well before the internet and I went door to door, selling from a magazine. Ding Dong, Avon Calling, that was me! I don't recall being nervous, just excited to be working for myself and making money. I was young but I enjoyed the ordering, bagging up the orders, and delivering the bag of goodies to my customers. It was a different and safer time.

8 Ways to Mind Your Own Business

Partnership

Partnerships are self-explanatory, you make the decision to partner with someone and you file the paperwork to create a company together. It might sound like a great way to share the expenses and workload, but remember, an entire specialty of the legal field is dedicated to partnerships. Some law firms do nothing else but dissolve partnerships. Ask yourself why that might be.

The scary truth is, partnerships rarely work out long term. It is not a question of WILL it go wrong but WHEN will it go wrong. If you decide to take this path, have a solid exit strategy in place (a written one) for when the time comes. Everyone thinks they will be the exception to the rule... most are not.

For many years as a business consultant, I preached of the dangers of partnerships. My mantra was NEVER have a partner. A few years ago, I decided I could be the exception to the rule, after all, I have years of business experience. The partnership was great for a couple of years, but one day my business partner walked away without explanation. A painful and expensive lesson learned.

Corporation

A corporation is an entity on its own, aside from you the owner of the corporation. You can change ownership of a corporation by buying or selling it, and the assets and liabilities follow the corporation. This is great news if you plan to build a company and then later sell it as your retirement or exit strategy. The corporate veil protects your own assets from lawsuits or other liabilities, which is the best reason to incorporate.

It is so easy to become incorporated; most states have a simple form you can fill out to register as a corporation. You can also hire a lawyer to do it for you, but I have never found it necessary.

Corporate Types

As a corporation, you will designate which type of corporation you would like to be. Limited Liability Company, standard Corporation, or an S-Corporation.

Many small business owners decide to be a Limited Liability Company or an LLC. This limits your own personal liability and can be a good choice if you will be a solo business owner, without employees, and just want a little extra protection for your assets. Just like the sole proprietor, income taxes are usually paid on your own social security number.

A standard corporation pay taxes on the company profits, remember it stands alone as an entity. One down-side to this is the double taxation that happens for the owner. The company earns money and pays taxes, and then the owner who draws a paycheck, also pays taxes. While that is usually seen as less than ideal, large companies function this way. The owners personal tax liability is based on the paycheck they take home.

The S-Corporation is just like the standard Corporate structure but with a huge benefit. The company earns money, but the profits pass through the company to the owner, who is then taxed at a lower rate. It offers all the protection of a standard corporation, but with the added benefit of no double taxation.

Over the years I have started, bought, or sold, and even given away, multiple business. Every company I have ever owned was a S-Corporation. That might not be the choice you make, and that's okay. For me, the benefit of the corporate veil and the flexibility of the S-corporation, made it my business structure of choice. You must decide what's right for you.

Each of the corporate structures we have discussed, will allow you to be a for profit or a not for profit company. The corporation comes first, then you can apply for a not for profit status if desired, and if your company will qualify.

A not for profit designation can be great if you intend to do charitable work, but it comes with a ton of paperwork and scrutiny. You are required to be 100% transparent to the taxing agencies and the public. Make sure you want that responsibility. Another option for charitable work is to create a foundation, AFTER you have a successful, for profit business.

Picking the right business structure for your company up front, will save you time and money later. The structure you chose for your business will determine how you will conduct business and pay your taxes. I always recommend consulting a professional before deciding.

While I am not familiar with countries outside the United States, I feel certain there is a local agency that has the answers, you just need to ask the right questions.

Taxes

None of us want to talk about taxes, but we must pay them. In the United States, we all pay federal taxes. Some states also have a state tax. Check with your local state for your requirements and be sure to learn about all your tax liabilities for your new company.

Keep in mind, as a self-employed person, YOU are the one paying social security and employment taxes. It is the price we pay for being a business owner I'm afraid.

Licensing

Licensing is another thing that is regulated at the state level. Professional licensing is very regulated, you probably know if you are required to be licensed for your line of work, but you might not realize you could need a business license as well.

8 Ways to Mind Your Own Business

Depending on your business type, your state might require a license at the state level AND a license at the county level, to do business. Non-compliance can lead to fines or even your business being shut down, which doesn't sound like fun to me. Check with your local state and county to be sure you're in compliance, better safe than sorry!

Benefits

Something else that new business owners need to consider is the lack of benefits. If your spouse or significant other provides you with benefits, you are blessed. They are expensive when you pay for them out of your pocket as a business owner, but peace of mind is well worth it.

Medical, dental, and life insurance, as well as workers compensation and your retirement plan, will now be funded by you. If you get sick or hurt, your benefits should not only cover your medical bills, but the time you are not able to work in your business. Take a minute to consider how you will handle your clients or customers if you are not able to work for a while. It makes sense to have a contingency plan for such an occasion.

Other insurance you might not have considered is professional or indemnity coverage. Of course, you will have general or public liability insurance on your business, we live in a very litigious time. People looking for quick money will sometimes target a business they perceive as having plenty of money to spare.

Depending on your business, you might also want Errors and Omission insurance. This will cover those services-based businesses and professionals who could inadvertently make a mistake or leave out something important, that might harm a client or customer. E&O insurance will help protect your business or professional license.

In this chapter we have talked about some topics that can be unnerving for a first-time business owner. Debbie will walk you through some discovery exercises you might find helpful during this process. Sticking your head in the sand or ignoring these things can bite you on the rear end later, if you're not careful. Do your due diligence, speak to the experts, and make good decisions for your new business.

If you are still with us, I know you have what it takes to make this happen.

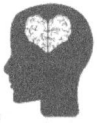

Inspired Business

You'll remember from an earlier chapter, cupping your hands in front of you and watching the seed of your intention germinate and start to grow. Seeing your ideas become reality is a wonderfully exciting time. Now as you see your seedling become stronger, you may be pulling out weeds of doubts and worries, whilst at the same time sorting out the practicalities of starting your business, which Clara has shared with you.

Where the initial germ of the idea to start your business journey was a wonderful internal adventure of the mind, now you may find, as you set about the logical practicalities, that there may be some challenges to overcome.

During what could be a very logical, intellectual phase of business development, it is a wonderful idea to maintain balance within your thinking. Know that no matter what challenges or difficulties you may encounter, you always have the choice to be gentle and loving to yourself. When you learn to go with the flow of life, rather than fight it, things seem so much easier.

The World According to You

During my studies in Spiritual Psychology, I was led to examine my life and become more consciously aware of how I was dealing with things. Looking back, I could see there were repeated patterns of behaviours and situations showing up. I hadn't realised it at the time, but life was giving me multiple opportunities to learn and grow, and I wasn't necessarily taking advantage of them.

I realised, so much of the difficulty I experienced in my life, could be traced back to an incident that happened three weeks after my fifteenth birthday.

That morning felt like any other. My dad had the day off work, so he offered to drive me the three miles to school, instead of me catching two buses. During the journey he complained of a pain in his left arm, and even asked me to change gear for him.

When I arrived at school, I gave him a kiss and a hug, and told him I would see him later… except I never did. He drove back home, told my mum he didn't feel well, sat down, and had a massive heart attack in her arms.

Yes, losing your dad is a pretty traumatic situation, and I found myself adrift afterwards. I was young and didn't know how to grieve. My friends didn't know what to say, so they kept their distance. It felt like my mum and I were ships drifting apart in the fog of hurt.

8 Ways to Mind Your Own Business

That one event changed my perception. I decided that I could only rely on me. I needed control over things in order to feel alright, and I couldn't necessarily count on other people to be there for me. It is interesting how events in our life create patterns of thinking and behaviours that we continue to use many years later.

So, control became a thing in my life. If I felt I could control a situation, I was alright. But if something happened outside my control, like a workplace restructure, I could feel fearful and dysfunctional.

The lesson I learnt during my Spiritual Psychology training was to let go of my need to have the world according to Debbie. I'm sharing this with you because you may be the same. My belief, for many years, was that life needed to unfold in the way I thought it should, otherwise I wouldn't be happy. I know the same is true for a lot of the people I speak to.

This is one of the greatest lessons I have learnt. To let go. To release the struggle of not having life turn out the way I think it should.

Notice I used the word should.

Should is such a powerful word, it gives us no get out clause and we feel trapped. To top it all off, it was my thinking that was putting the pressure there.

So, if you are feeling the pressure of having your business unfold in a certain way, let go of that need. Allow yourself to feel safe no matter what is going on around you. Know that you can handle any situation.

For me, it was all about a lack of belief in myself. As I became aware of my dysfunction; and started learning to trust myself and life, things became easier. It is all about becoming consciously aware and having the courage to change.

How you Deal with Life's Challenges

As your business evolves and the practicalities of running your business kick in, you will no doubt encounter times when things are challenging. How you approach and deal with them, will be according to what you have learnt to this point in your life.

Sometimes the same types of challenges keep showing up, because we haven't learnt the lessons, they are showing us. We have approached them with our old thinking, then wondered why things aren't working. So, I would like to invite you to do an exercise with me.

If you are in a safe place to do so, I would like to ask you to close your eyes. Otherwise, just follow the exercise in your imagination as best you can.

Now, I would like you to take a deep breath in, hold it for a few seconds, and then release it out slowly. Repeat this again allowing that wonderful diaphragm to relax you, and as you do so, take your awareness from whatever is going on in your mind, and place it on your breath.

With the next deep breath in, imagine following the breath around your body, providing that wonderful life force… and then breathing out all you no longer need.

Bringing your breathing back to its normal and natural rhythm, I would like you to imagine that you are inside a container of some sort. A container with a lid.

As you look around, check in with yourself, and ask yourself how you feel about being in there? What is it like in there? What is your position? How much room do you have?

Then pay attention to what the container is made of. Note its colour and shape.

Now get out of the container in any way you can, and once you have done so, open your eyes.

I want you to know that there is no right or wrong way to do this… whatever way you do it, is right for you.

If you have time it would be really useful for you to be able to write in your journal your experience of this exercise. Otherwise just mull it over in your mind, commit it to memory, and make a note of it later.

Now I would like you to reflect on how you felt in the container. Did you feel cramped? Or did you have room to move around? Did you feel trapped? Or safe?

What was your container made of? Was it a light material like paper or cardboard? Or was it something heavier like wood, metal, or stone?

When I asked you to get out of it, what was that like for you? Was it easy? Did it seem too easy, so you made the journey more difficult? Did you stay trapped inside and not manage to get out at all? Or did you jump out and want to climb straight back in?

As I said there are no right or wrong answers, but your experience will reveal to you how your subconscious mind deals with challenges. If you see challenges as a gift, then your container may have presented itself as a gift box. If you deal with challenges in a light way then your container will have been made of light material, maybe fabric, paper, or cardboard. If you see challenges as something much more difficult to deal with, your container will be made of heavier material, like stone, wood, or metal. If you see your challenges as killing you, your box may've been a coffin.

If you got out easily, then you feel equipped to get out of challenges easily. If you remained trapped, then you are likely to feel like you get trapped in your difficulties.

It is interesting, and helpful, to know how you deal with challenges subconsciously. It doesn't matter what the outcome was. The way you deal with challenges in this moment has been formed from past experiences. It is learnt behaviour.

Now you have the most amazing and wonderful choice to change, if you want to. Know that you no longer need to be defined by past thinking. You can create new ways of thinking and doing. Know you can see any challenges you may be facing or experiencing with your business as something you can deal with easy and effortlessly. You have all the tools within you to handle any situation.

In essence, how you think and perceive challenges is everything. Realise that your perception has been created by you, so you have the power to see things differently.

Stepping out in the right direction

You may have experienced times before when you reached a cross-road in life and didn't know which direction to take. You may have even experienced this with your fledgling business. If you have, here are some things to do, to help you keep stress and doubt from creeping in.

Firstly, bring your attention back to your breath. Put one hand on your belly and the other on your chest and breathe. As you breathe normally and naturally, pay attention to which hand is moving more. Often, when we feel stressed, anxious, or unsure, our breathing can become shallow and up in the chest.

If you are feeling that now, the hand on your chest will be moving more than the hand on your belly. Consciously breathe deeper and allow the breath to reach and expand your belly.

Allow yourself to bring your attention to your breath. Continuing this practice for a few minutes will help to centre and ground you, which will enable you to get a better perspective on the situation.

Another way you can gain clarity on your direction is to reach for your journal and write. There are different ways you can approach this. You can either flow write how you feel about the situation. Or you can pose yourself a question and see what answer comes forth as you write. You can even write yourself a letter from either the older, wiser part of yourself, or from someone you really admire, whose opinion you value.

Journaling really is a great way to explore who you are, what you believe, and help you to gain clarity on your direction going forward.

It may seem easier to just ask your friends, family, and trusted advisors for advice on your next steps… and yes, these can be helpful if you want a technical piece of advice. However, what you might not be doing is giving yourself the time to explore the situation yourself.

The people around us are, on the whole, well-meaning and will provide oodles of advice. So, if you asked one hundred people what they think you should do, you will no doubt end up with a huge array of different answers, and still feel none-the-wiser about your next steps.

No matter how well-meaning these people are, they do not know what is in your highest best interest. Only you do. Which is why I have suggested journaling because this is a form of listening to yourself and seeking that inner wisdom within.

Another way of finding the right direction for you, especially if you are a visual person, is through the following use of imagery.

Your Path of Discovery

So, let's say that you have a decision to make in your new business, and at the moment you can see two different paths to take. You may feel so caught up in having to make a decision that your head is full of noise and lack of clarity. Therefore, you may not be able to clearly distinguish the right way forward.

If you are in this situation, this exercise will be really helpful to you. If you can do this when you are sitting in a quiet spot with your eyes closed, do it, allow yourself the time. If it is not safe to close your eyes right now, don't worry. Follow this exercise in your imagination and it will still reveal things to you that will help.

Start this journey of discovery with moving your awareness from what is going on in your mind and placing it on your breath. Then feel the rise and fall of your belly as each breath centres and grounds you. With each out breath feel your body relax a little more.

Now, in your mind I want you to imagine you are walking along a path. The scenery to either side of you is lovely and it feels such a safe place to be. Up ahead you see a group of people, and as you near them they start to crowd around you, giving you their opinion as to what they think you should do.

Although you know they have the best of intentions, the noise feels overwhelming. It is too much, and you can hardly hear yourself think. So, you pull away from them, and as the noise subsides you see just ahead a fork in the road.

Reaching the fork, you stop and look in one direction, then the other, not sure which path to take. In your mind think of one of your potential solutions forking off to the left, and the other solution forking to the right. As you don't yet know which of your solutions is the right one… you will try both out to see.

In your mind you take the left-hand path and follow it along its twists and turns, until you reach a door. Reaching for the handle you pause for a moment, then open the door.

As you step in and close the door behind you, you find your first solution playing out around you. You are now part of that journey.

Allow this mind movie to play out and take notice of what is going on around you. Note how you feel. Pay attention to any thoughts you may be thinking. Really feel you are part of the movie and see yourself acting out your role.

Keep paying attention to your thoughts and feelings as the mind movie plays out all the way to its completion. Does it play out the way you had thought? Or do other things happen?

When you feel your journey on this path has finished, walk back to the door, open it and close it behind you. Trust that everything you needed to know about that solution was revealed to you.

Now follow the path back towards the fork in the road. As you stand there facing the right-hand fork in the road, bring your second solution to mind.

When you feel ready to, set off along that path, paying attention to how this path compares with the other. Is it straighter, or does it have more twists and turns? Once again, you eventually reach a door. How does this door compare to the one on the other path? Is it old, or new? Is it ugly or beautiful? Reaching out for the handle you pause for a moment, then open it.

As you step in and close the door, you find your second solution playing out around you. And you are now part of that journey.

See what is going on around you. Pay attention to how you feel, including any thoughts you may be thinking. Really feel that you are part of the movie and see yourself acting out your role.

Keep paying attention to your feelings as the mind movie plays out all the way to the completion. Does it play out the way you had thought? Or do other things happen?

When you feel that your journey on this path has finished, walk back to the door, open it, and close it behind you. Trust that everything you needed to know about that solution was revealed to you.

Once again make your way back to the fork in the road. As you reach there looking from one path to the other. What did these journeys reveal to you? What did you learn that you didn't know before? Which path felt right to take?

If you feel compelled to write your experience in your journal, do so. I have always found this exercise really revealing. There have been times when my intellect was telling me the left-hand path would be the right course of action. Yet, when I did this exercise, I knew instinctively that the other path was right for me.

In doing this exercise you are tapping into something greater than your intellect or your ego… you are tapping into that innate pool of wisdom within you, which knows the right next steps of your journey.

Inspired Business

As you move along your business journey to creating the success and life you want, know that the answers you seek are always within you. A business built from the basis of inspiration has a much stronger and deeper foundation than one built on the intellect alone.

8 Ways to Mind Your Own Business

Trust that the help, support, and answers you seek along the way will be revealed to you. Let go of the struggle, the need to know everything now, and trust life will unfold perfectly. Know that there is an inspired answer to any business challenge you may be facing. The right people will be attracted into your life at the right time.

So, when you feel your intuition telling you to do something, do it. Even if you don't understand why, trust it. For you might be led to the answer you are seeking.

8 Ways to Mind Your Own Business

 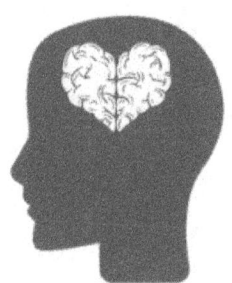

4th Way

Operation MATTERS

When you first dreamed about starting your business, I'd be willing to bet that creating forms and tools, was not part of the vision. By now, I hope your vision has grown as your dream comes to life.

During our previous chapter on creative matters, we talked about the company name, logo, and color palette of your brand. There are still more decisions to be made related to those creative pieces, I like to call them marketing tools.

Tools

While it doesn't sound like an operations issue, marketing is a part of business operations. Don't be overwhelmed by the word. Marketing is the word used to describe the words, pictures, and messages you use to connect with your potential customers, both on your website and in print.

If you have a flair for the creative, there are great tools you can use to design and create your own marketing materials. I personally use Canva, Publisher, and PowerPoint, for most of my marketing materials. I caution you, if this is NOT in your comfort zone, find a professional to help you. Your marketing materials are some of the tools you will use to attract your customers. Don't be the newbie that prints their own cards on perforated stock, it screams unprofessional.

How the world see's your business, matters, so your marketing message and tools need to be consistent, concise, and professional.

Domain Name

Gone are the days when a business could get by without an online presence. Before you run out and hire a web developer, start by purchasing your own domain name. I like to get my domain names from GoDaddy, but there are other online sources to purchase one.

If your business name is available as a domain name, it's probably a good choice. It is how people will find you online. In fact, you might have already considered this when naming your company. If your company name is not available, find a creative way to say what your business does, and buy that domain name.

Think about how a potential customer might search for your business. If they don't know about you, and they don't know your company name, what key words will they use in the search engine?

Pick something relevant to your business, remember our conversation about picking a good name! Your domain name will also become part of

8 Ways to Mind Your Own Business

your professional email address so it should make sense and not be confusing. Of course, the domain name should be consistent with your company branding.

A good example of creative domain names; is my own business. My business name WAS available but apparently it was so good that GoDaddy priced it for sale at $30,000.00 for the first year, and I was not ready to plunk down that kind of cash on a domain name! So instead, I purchased CraftingYourMessage and CreatingYourBook for about $15.00 each, and I use them for my website and platform.

Anytime I have a great idea for a new product, I hop over to GoDaddy to find a great name. SAVVY Business Builders was one I used right away after purchasing it BUT Influence Builders was a name I grabbed long before I used it to build the online community it is today. Sometimes I end up using the name, other times I don't and eventually let the domain name expire. Either way, it is a small cost that I am willing to pay.

The most important thing to know is that you want to be the OWNER of your domain name, because it gives you complete control over it. Trust me, you don't want a web developer or consultant owning your domain, and then holding it hostage or going out of business and disappearing. I have had clients who had been paying hundreds of dollars a year for their domain name, simply because they didn't know better. It happens more than you think, own your tools as much as possible.

Website

At a minimum, you will need a website that acts as a brochure about your business, this saves you time by educating clients about your products or services. It is where you will convey a professional and reliable image of your company.

Your website can also do some of the work FOR you by providing information about the company vision and mission, keep in touch through regular blog posts, and even offer a place to schedule appointments. Your website is an extension of your business, pay attention to this important part of your marketing.

Again, I recommend having a website that you have complete control over. I like a self-hosted WordPress site, but a paid platform can also work, if you maintain complete control over it. If someone else can shut down your site for any reason, you don't have control.

Headshots

Over the years as a consultant, I have seen some great marketing tools ruined by a few simple things, but the most common is the do it yourself headshot. You know the ones I'm talking about, where someone stands in front of a white wall and has their friend or spouse take a picture.

Often new business owners are reluctant to spend the money on professional headshots. This is a huge mistake. Even with the great camera on our smart phone, nothing compares to the eye and lighting of a professional. Spend a little money on this, a great headshot can last you several years and pays for itself in professionalism.

Systems

Once the marketing tools are created, it is time to focus on the organizational side of operations for your business. These are the systems that create continuity and efficiency while serving your customers.

The day to day activities that happen in your new business will be time consuming. If you don't have established systems to keep you organized, things will fall through the cracks and get overlooked. Now is the time to create the tools for smooth and effective operation of your business.

I like to think about this part of operations in a linear way, from the start of the customer experience to the end. If you haven't done so yet, take a few minutes to map out what that looks like in your business.

The customer journey is every interaction your business has with a customer, from start to finish. Imagine you are your customer, learning about your business for the first time. Where did they find you? What did your marketing message say to them? How did they contact you? What did you say to them? How did you serve them? I could go step by step through the journey, but you get the idea.

Forms

With this map in hand, start creating the forms you will need to track your customer through the customer journey. Each step on the map represents another form, file, or follow up system, you will need to create.

In my business, my first internal form is a client intake form, it lets me gather information on a new client, or potential client, in a consistent manner. I don't need to remember what information I want from them; I simply fill out the form as we chat. By doing this, I always have the information I need, and my clients are each treated the same.

As a bonus to using forms, if I need to outsource a task to an assistant, there is a well-established system to follow.

Files

While not a very exciting topic to discuss, well organized files are worth their weight in gold. You will need files for the legal paperwork, for the account receivables and payables, for vendors and employees, and much more.

All you need is plenty of file folders and a label maker, and a consistent plan for filing things where they belong. Countless times, good filing habits have saved my skin!

8 Ways to Mind Your Own Business

Follow Up

No doubt you have heard the phrase, "The fortune is in the follow up." It's a well-known saying because it holds a kernel of truth.

As you start to network or talk to new potential customers, you will need a consistent follow up system. There are great online tools available if you like technology, but the old-fashioned day planner will work as well.

It can be as simple as setting a reminder on your calendar or having separate inboxes for files you need to follow up on. The important part is having a consistent method for following up on the money trail that is comfortable for you.

Gratitude

Your success in business will have a direct correlation to your level of gratitude. You will always get more from those who feel appreciated, it's human nature.

Thank your customers often, without them you don't have a business. I like to send thank you cards and personal emails, expressing my appreciation for their business. This is a great time to ask for feedback and referrals or reviews.

Your business will continue to grow through referrals from happy customers. When you get a referral, treat it like the precious thing it is.

First, thank the person that did the referring! After all, you want them to do it again right!?! They will feel good when you thank them, and they will be more likely to send you more referrals.

Then, take great care of that new referral, they will probably report back to the person who referred them! If you fail here, you won't get another referral from that source, and you have missed an opportunity to create another satisfied customer.

Don't forget to thank your vendors, the businesses you purchase goods and services from, think of them as partners in your business. Send holiday cards or small gifts with a note, it can make a real difference in the service you receive from them.

We don't want to forget about our employees and contractors either. These people will be in the trenches each day, helping you grow your business and service your customers. They need to know you appreciate their efforts and hard work.

If I could only give you one piece of advice, to impact your business, it would be to always show gratitude toward those who make your success possible.

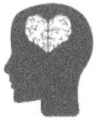

Inspired Operations

When we think of operations it is easy to sit down and create a long list of things to do. As Clara explained, there will be tasks you'll want to complete, processes you want to put into place, and photos and wording you want on your website. When we get into the head space of sorting out the business operations, it is easy for our thought processes to be completely driven by logic and reason.

It can seem like there is a never-ending stream of tasks and things to do, that keep making their way on to your task list. It can feel like you are never going to get to the end of it. Your mind can feel crowded. You can feel overwhelmed. You may feel like no matter how much you do, there never seems to be enough time to do everything you want to do.

If you feel like that, know you aren't alone. Know that there is a better way.

Operating from a Place of Inspired Action

Remembering back to the time when I was a corporate employee, I always had a to-do list as long as my arm. No matter how hard I worked, it never seemed to get any shorter. There came a time when I felt I was like a hamster in a wheel, running, but never really getting anywhere.

If you feel like that too... know you are not alone. It may feel like you are going no-where fast.

The difficulty in this type of approach is we get caught up in DOING mode. We feel the only effort that is worthwhile is when we are being active... writing reports, building websites, having meetings, building contacts, creating processes, landing pages, opt in forms, lead magnets... and the list goes on and on.

Although taking action is good, there comes a point when we are moving forward, but only from the place of doing what we think we should be doing. It is all coming from logic and ego. Logic tells us we need to build a mailing list and a website, we need to have a strategy, a vision, and a business plan, amongst other things. Ego tell us that we need to be faster and accomplish more. We need to write perfect copy and know the perfect thing to say at the perfect time. In short, ego tells us we aren't good enough... and no matter what we do, it will never be satisfied.

It sounds horrendous, and it doesn't leave you feeling good either. There is so much pressure. Not only from imposed deadlines, or self-imposed deadlines, but also the words you use. Most of the pressure you feel, you have created yourself.

8 Ways to Mind Your Own Business

I am going to share a better way with you. It may seem a bit strange and go against the grain but go with it. The lesson I have learnt is that just because we are taking action and seemingly productive, it doesn't mean we are taking the right action. We could be, unknowingly, going down any number of wrong rabbit holes. When we are so caught up in the moment of doing, we don't see the danger signs. So, we waste time and effort doing things that don't really need to be done.

There is an old saying, time is money. It makes us think we need to be doing something in order to feel productive. Yet that doesn't mean we need to be physically doing something. How about inner work and contemplation, does that not count?

Actually, taking time out to reflect on where you are, and contemplating on the next right steps for you to take, is an incredibly valuable way of moving forward. To some, it may seem like not working. Yet it is. Let me explain.

Know there is always a stream of inspiration flowing through you. Call it your intuition, your gut feeling, whatever you'd like. Your intuition is your guiding light, helping you to move in the right direction. The problem comes when your head is so full of things to do, you don't even hear your intuition. That leaves you following ego and logic, and potentially expending more energy than you need to. If you had listened to your intuition, you would be taking inspired action instead. Your inspiration is telling you exactly what the right next step is. You only need to listen.

Tapping into your Inspiration

Your inspiration is the life force within you, and it will always lead you in the right direction. Many years ago, when I was on the path to becoming an Accountant, I tuned out my intuition, instead of listening to it. I had the feeling I was doing the wrong thing, yet I ignored it. I didn't take action on its warnings. It wasn't long before I regretted my career choice. My logical thinking, which I had placed my trust in, had led me in the wrong direction, and I was unhappy.

Yet my intuition had known my choice was wrong all along.

Listening to your inner guidance may come easy for you, or it may take time to tune into again. You may already trust it, or it may take a while to build up that trust, especially if you were like me and had tuned it out.

I recommend you start to spend some time each day, in silence, sitting with your eyes closed. If you don't already do this, you will find it a great way to de-clutter your thinking. With your eyes closed allow your awareness to move off whatever is going on in your mind and place it on your breath. You could pay attention to the rise and fall of your belly as you breathe, or the feeling of the air as it comes in and out of your nostrils.

When a thought pops into your head, and it will, gently and lovingly release the thought and allow your awareness to rest back on to your breathing.

8 Ways to Mind Your Own Business

You can start by allocating maybe five minutes a day to this practice, and increase it over time, until you reach twenty or thirty minutes. To which you may say, I don't have twenty or thirty spare minutes a day to do that! If you are thinking that, trust me. Tuning into your intuition will save you a lot of time, effort and maybe even money, when you listen to it.

When you do this practice every day, you gradually quieten the mind, so you can hear your intuition. Then, you can also take questions within, or find out whether your beliefs are keeping you in a place of procrastination and not moving forward. In fact, you can seek guidance on anything you care to ask yourself.

Another way you can access your intuition is through free-flow journaling. Free flowing means to write without stopping. One way you can do this is through writing a letter to yourself from either the older wiser part of you, or from someone whose opinion you trust, it doesn't matter whether you actually know them. In this way you seem to by-pass the mind and access some deeper wisdom within you. I find I gain a deeper understanding of the situation, a new perspective, and even inspiration on a way forward, through journaling.

In doing either of these exercises, you will find your level of trust in yourself will increase. That you will instinctively know the right thing to do, instead of looking outside of yourself for the answers. You will know which contacts are right to make, or the right contracts to take, and the right clients to sign up, and so forth.

When I started practicing this, it took me a while to trust my feelings. To know whether it was my intuition, and not just my imagination, or my ego talking. Yes, I have made some mistakes along the way. But overall trust in my judgement has increased. My stress levels have decreased dramatically too. I am now less inclined to reach out to others for their opinion. My work has a calmness about it, and I feel an immense amount of inner peace. Overall, I am more productive than I was, with much less effort.

You can use this technique for the benefit of others too.

Your Customer's Journey

To have a successful business, you will need customers. You will want to provide goods or services which are of value to them. You will also want to make it easy for them to buy from you. When you are in DOING mode, you may think the processes, systems, and procedures you are creating are with the customer in mind. However, you might be missing a trick by not allowing yourself to experience it from their point of view.

This is where the process of looking within can really make a huge difference to your business.

What I do is to sit comfortably, close my eyes and then think of myself as one of my customers.

8 Ways to Mind Your Own Business

My clients have different channels in which they can access my services, depending on whether they want one to one coaching, workshops, or an online programme. So, I take one of them, say, my online programmes, and then I visualise how a customer will find them. I start by imagining how the advertising looks to them. Then I see them clicking through to the sales page, and then the checkout, paying attention to how this process feels. Then I visualise myself using my own programme. I pay attention to how it looks and feels. Was it easy to purchase, to access and use?

You can use this technique for all types of situations. You can even adapt it to use during meetings, or at networking events, or even for creating physical products. All you need to do is visualise the situation from the other point of view. Actually, the application of this technique is endless.

As you do this exercise feel gratitude for the insights this process is giving you. For the business you are creating, for the customers you have or will have, for the help and support you are attracting, for the money you are making, and for the difference you are making to your clients.

I always find it helps to write things to feel grateful about in your journal. Gratitude is a really important area and one we'll be covering in more detail in a later chapter.

This exercise will help you to see things with a new perspective. To really put yourself in the shoes of your clients and prospective clients. Give it a go and see how much insight it gives you. It will really help you to create a great customer experience.

De-Cluttering

So far, you have discovered how valuable de-cluttering your thinking is, now, I would like you to apply this to your actual environment.

In your mind, think about the place in which you work. Allow the picture to form in your imagination, or if you are actually there, look around. What does it look like? What does it feel like being in that place?

Is it tidy or cluttered?

Your environment has an effect upon your thinking. If your surroundings are cluttered while you creatively construct your new business, it will have an impact on how cluttered your thinking is.

I am not suggesting you need to work in a minimalist environment, but it really does help if your workplace is orderly. Otherwise you will be trying to de-clutter your thinking, and your work environment will be fighting against that.

So, if your work area is cluttered, why is it? Is it because you are not using technology efficiently? Or, because you don't have enough physical storage?

If you want your business operations to run smoothly, along with your thinking, you will want your workspace to be organised too.

If it is, that's great. If it isn't, what can you commit to doing to create the calm, peaceful, organised, and professional environment which will support your thinking and your business? Know that spending time to de-clutter now, will help you to be more productive going forward. Clutter really is a big-time waster.

Getting in your own way

So far, we have talked about how cluttered thinking and a cluttered environment can get in our way. We have talked about spending time getting back in connection with our inspiration, in order to know the right next course of action to take, and to see how our decisions are impacting our clients and customers. Yet there is still one thing that can get in your way... and that is YOU.

When you are creating inspired operations for your business you will be aware of the strategies, processes, and other things you need to put into place in order for your successful business to be created. So, I will ask you this... are you actually putting these things into place? If not, why not?

A business coach friend of mine told me recently, that he got frustrated when he gave his clients information about what to do, then when he went to see them a month later, they hadn't done it. Nor had they done it the month after that.

Why is it that we know what to do, yet don't do it?

Actually, I'll tell you... it comes down to our beliefs. We covered this a bit in the Inspired Passion chapter, when you looked at your beliefs around success, failure, work, financial prosperity, and fulfilment.

If you remember, our beliefs can be so engrained we don't always realise how much they are controlling our actions and behaviours. When we are given a piece of information to follow to ensure success, if we don't believe at a deep level that we are worthy of success, then we will procrastinate. We will hold ourselves back, subconsciously.

I would like to invite you to think about whether you catch yourself saying any of the following:

Running a successful business would be great, but...

I can't do that piece of work, or have a successful business because...

I should...

I'm not...

When you hear yourself saying something along those lines, it is a wonderful indicator that you have a belief getting in the way. When you have that realisation feel grateful, for now you have the choice to change. Change starts with altering the language you use, both in your self-talk and to other people.

8 Ways to Mind Your Own Business

The Choice to Change

You really do have the choice to change. You can believe your business will be a success. That you will attract the right clients, prosperity, contracts, accountant, funding source, website designer, and anything else you feel you may need. That you can create an amazing customer journey for your clients.

The way you choose to think, and what you believe is possible, is everything. Observe your thoughts to see if they control you, or whether you are in control of your thinking. Remember the Push Me Pull You I told you about in an earlier chapter. The words you use either move you towards, or away from what you want.

One of the easy ways to start training your thinking is through the use of affirmations. These are simple active language statements which affirm what you want, as if you already have it.

I always suggest to my clients that they compile a few sentences which they can use when they become aware their thinking is not supporting their journey.

For example, instead of saying, *I'm never going to get this done,* you could replace that with, *I know that everything is accomplished with ease and effortlessness.*

The new words may seem strange and untrue but keep saying them. Don't just repeat the words, say them with feeling. You are using the feeling you create to change your belief. So, use present tense, active language, as if what you want to do or be is already here.

I've heard clients on numerous occasions say something like, I'm stupid. When really what they mean is their actions were stupid. There is a big difference there.

Recognizing how you speak to yourself is important, you won't change by berating yourself. You change through positive, nourishing, and supportive language.

As you set up the operations side of your business, be aware of the language you use. Be gentle and loving to yourself. Know that you and your customers deserve the best in life. Listen to your gut feeling and take inspired action, rather than doing something because you think you should be doing it. De-clutter your thinking at the same time as you declutter your work environment.

Finally, feel gratitude in knowing that everything is unfolding perfectly and that all will be well.

8 Ways to Mind Your Own Business

 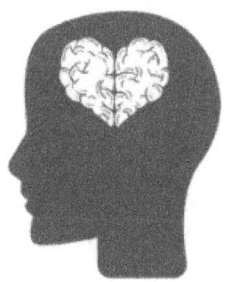

5th Way

8 Ways to Mind Your Own Business

Prosperity MATTERS

Let's talk about Prosperity. We can all agree, starting your own business is exciting, often the dream has been brewing in your mind for years. Depending on your personality you may have spent time dreaming about calling your own shots, or you might have envisioned the difference you would make for your clients or customers. Whatever your dreams have looked like, no doubt it included making money and becoming prosperous.

What is prosperity, really? I've heard it described as thriving or flourishing, which usually comes with a social status of successful. The interesting thing is this, success looks different, to different people. So, while money and prosperity are not the same thing, money is required for business prosperity.

The topic of money is not always a comfortable one for new business owners. Of course, you must have revenue coming in for your new business to survive. For many of us, we also need to provide for our personal or family needs as well. It's not enough for your new business to make money, YOU must make money as well. You can't pay your bills with smiles and good intentions.

Comfort level aside, as a new business owner, you need to find a way to get comfortable with the basics on these subjects: your pricing, cash flow, budgeting, and even business funding. So, we are going to spend a little time defining them and going over the fundamentals.

Pricing

It starts with believing, in the value of what you offer. You researched this during your due diligence, you did the work, now trust yourself.

In business we all offer a product or service in exchange for money, or sometimes goods or services, but primarily it is intended to produce revenue. Revenue that will sustain and grow your new business. Unless you have some experience with pricing, it can be intimidating. You don't want to charge too much and price yourself out of the market, but you also need to make an actual profit.

The first thing to understand about pricing is, you never want to get involved in the race to the bottom. That is to say… you don't want to play the "Mine is cheaper" game. No one really wins, and you will only attract those customers who are looking for the best deal. Instead, look for ways to add value to what you offer. What can you include that makes your pricing the BETTER deal? There is always something you can include that will add value, making your price the obviously better option. Don't forget to consider your unique selling point, it can impact your pricing as well.

8 Ways to Mind Your Own Business

A good rule of thumb for a physical product is to buy it at cost, then double that for the retail price. If the product costs you ten dollars, you sell it for twenty dollars, and the mark up of ten dollars is your profit. Included in that profit is your overhead, a part of your cost of doing business.

For those who sell a service, as I do, pricing is determined by the value of your time and offering. First decide what your time is worth per hour. (Not as if you were an employee taking home a check, this is different. You ARE the employer now and will cover all the expenses). Take the amount of time the service will require of you and do the math. If your hourly rate is two hundred dollars, clients can hire you by the hour or you can offer package deals that save them money. You might consider a five-hour package for five hundred dollars, what a great saving for your customer! Offering several pricing options will allow your clients to pick a package at their own comfort level.

In my business, many of the services require some of my time, but also require my clients time and efforts as well. So, I have created packages, that include specific activities or outcomes.

For instance, when I work with clients who are writing their book, I spend time with them brainstorming and blueprinting the outline of their book. We strategize what they will do with the completed book, and then they spend time writing the content. Afterwards, I spend time editing the content, and finally formatting and publishing the book. Tracking the time on the project would be time consuming, it's just easier to charge a package price for co-writing their book with them. This is a much greater value to my clients, but I still get paid for my time.

If you're fortunate enough to have BOTH products and services in your new business, it will take a bit a time to create your pricing structure. Settle on what feels right, but don't spend too much time fussing about this. Get paid what you are worth, keeping in mind what the market will bear.

Business is fluid, there is an ebb and flow to it. Over time your customer's needs will help shape and change your business and your pricing. That's okay, it's normal. All successful businesses continually grow and change, to stay relevant.

Remember, the sale of your product or service is about revenue for your entire business. All your overhead, or business expenses, are also covered by your sales. This is the perfect time to talk about your budget and cash flow!

Budgeting

Now there's a term that will excite some people and bring a wave a nausea to others. Depending on your view about money and spending, this could be fun, or it could be brutal.

The number crunchers and analytical minds have been sweating through the creative process of starting a business, but now they are feeling more at ease. If this is you, welcome home! Enjoy the process of creating the perfect budget that accounts for all the expenses of running a successful business.

Take heart if you are a creative, who would rather crawl through broken glass than create and follow a budget, it is not as hard as it sounds. It's simply a projection of money in and money out, for your new business.

Budgeting is designed to anticipate cash flow; cash flow in… and cash flow out. This might be obvious but start by making a list of every potential income source for your new business and every probable expense for operating your business.

PRO Tip: When you consider potential revenue, look for ways to create a variety of low-ticket and high-ticket sources. If your business is selling a product, look for a related service you could also sell to your customer at the same time. If you sell a service, what product could you create to complement the service and create another revenue source?

Take some time to really brainstorm all your potential expenses. Imagine yourself working in your business, what activities are you doing? Where are you doing them? What tools or resources will you need to purchase or pay monthly for? How much will your products or services cost you? Don't forget things such as shipping and postage, office supplies, gas, networking expenses, and costs of professional association memberships.

Create a month by month chart or table, to track your expenses and then add any debt repayments. When you consider all potential expenses, then you will know how much revenue you need to bring in to cover those expenses AND still make a profit you can take home.

A budget will not be perfect, remember it's a projection for planning purposes. It will give you guidance when considering new expenditures. Can your business afford the new computer or iPhone you're drooling over? Check with your budget.

You've probably heard the term Robbing Peter to pay Paul, and it can be a devastating trap for the new business owner. Budgeting can help ensure you are better prepared for the inconsistency of cash flow, that is a normal part of doing business. Think of your budget as a tool to keeping your spending in check, and your business finances on track.

A solid, well planned budget will be a necessary tool, if you need outside funding for your new business.

Funding MATTERS

Over the years I have owned multiple businesses. Most of them were self-funded start-ups, but a couple did require some funding. It can be daunting to find and obtain a funding source for your new start-up, not every funding source is willing to take a chance on a new business.

8 Ways to Mind Your Own Business

Self-funding or bootstrapping a new business is possible for most service-based businesses. You will still need funds, but your savings can usually handle the basic costs of getting started. Most of the time you can have a home-based office, which cuts down significantly on the overhead expenses. If you will have a store front with physical products, outside funding is probably necessary.

At least in the United States, retail space is leased by the square footage, and usually has additional expenses, sometimes called triple net. As a tenant, you will pay a portion of the owner's taxes, insurance, and maintenance expenses, it is added on top of the square foot price for the space. These additional expenses will change from year to year, as the building owner's expenses change.

Most store front property will also need to be modified to accommodate your specific business needs. While those expenses belong to you, it can be a negotiation tool during the leasing process. Most owners will pitch in for the renovations for a longer lease agreement. Do your research before jumping into a location and a long-term lease! Location, location, location… is a big consideration BUT don't forget to protect yourself during the lease process. It is easy to get excited about the new adventure and get into a lease you later regret. Please read your lease and ask a professional any questions, if you don't understand something

If you decide funding is a necessity, start at your chamber of commerce or Small Business Association, for local resources. Talk to your community bank or credit union, they are often business friendly, with programs for new businesses. Some counties have economic development councils, with low interest loans designed to encourage new businesses and economic growth. They are usually NOT tied to your credit and have lower interest rates then you will get elsewhere.

Getting outside funding can feel unnerving, as you are starting your new business adventure with debt. I am not saying you shouldn't obtain funding if you need it, just be smart about it. Your budgeting will give you the necessary information you will need for borrowing. It includes the correct amount to meet your start up needs, as well as the expenses of the early months in your new business when revenue is slow.

Whenever possible, I would choose to self-fund a new business, but if you are getting funding, know your comfort level for debt and your borrowing limits.

I trust you are still with me and feeling more confident about your progress on your business. We still have a couple of topics to cover but you are almost ready to serve that first customer!

With your pricing set, a budget projection done, and the funding decision made, you will be ready to start attracting your customers. Those customers who will bring the revenue and have you on your way to business prosperity and success, no matter how you define it.

Inspired Prosperity

As Clara mentioned, the topic of money is always a very interesting one and is often tied up with a lot of emotion. Discussions about money can be even more emotive than those about sex.

So, what are your beliefs about money? Do you find that it flows easily and effortlessly into your life? Does it flow out, as quickly as it flows in? Or does acquiring it always feel like a struggle?

The interesting thing is, when we think about acquiring greater levels of prosperity, money has nothing to do with financial freedom.

The Difference between Money and Wealth

Many people believe that money is tied to wealth, except it isn't really. When we talk about money and wealth, we are talking about two different things.

Money is a commodity which we use to barter for goods and services. It is a tool which we can use. Yet, for many people it is a tool which rules their lives. Did you know, apparently nine out of ten people work just for money? Yes, we need money to live, but do you think this is the only reason we should work? How about working with the focus of creating peace, harmony, and the ability to creatively express yourself?

If money is a commodity, what is wealth? Aren't they one and the same thing? The answer is no, they aren't. Wealth is different because it is a mind-set.

I can remember watching a programme on the television where a man travelling around different countries was looking for the kindness of others to put him up for the night and pay for his food. During one of his overnight stops, he bumped into a man and got chatting. On asking the man if he could put him up for the night, the traveller was surprised to find the man was homeless. Even though the man had virtually nothing, he led the traveller to the place where was going to sleep and shared his bedding, his clothing, his food, and even the small amount of money he had with him.

Even though he had hardly anything to call his own, he didn't hold onto it, he was willing to share. What the homeless man didn't know was that the traveller was giving gifts of kindness, to those he felt were deserving. Of course, the homeless man received a wonderfully generous gift of financial help to kick start the building of a new life for himself.

Even though the homeless man had very little money, he hadn't shown a poverty consciousness. In fact, his mind-set had been one of wealth, for he had been able to share the little he had with others.

8 Ways to Mind Your Own Business

There are stories at the other end of the spectrum too. There is one story I heard, and I have no idea whether it is true or some kind of moral tale, but I will share it with you here, because I think it helps to illustrate a different mind-set and how it can impact your life.

It is told that there was once a couple, who over their lifetime amassed a huge fortune. It was more money than they could ever spend, and because they were incredibly fearful of being poor, they were frugal with spending the money and hoarded it away, just in case they might need it in the future.

After many years of thrifty spending, they built a large vault on their estate, in which to store their amassed fortune and keep it safe. Instead of enjoying their wealth and sharing it with others, they kept it locked up and protected, afraid that at any time it would be taken away from them.

One day they heard that a gang of thieves were in the neighbourhood, and the couple became frightened. What if the robbers broke into their home! What if they found the money and stole it all! As far as they were concerned, that would be the end of their world.

To allay their fears and feel secure, the couple decided to check on their vault and make sure all was safe. Making their way to the vault, they opened up the great strong door, and stepped inside. They breathed a sigh of relief when they saw that all their carefully saved money was still intact. However, as they turned to leave, the big heavy vault door swung shut. They were trapped.

With no-one knowing they were there, and no way for them to escape the fortress they had built to protect their money, they remained trapped and never managed to escape.

Where the homeless man had a prosperity consciousness, the old couple protecting their fortune, were trapped in a poverty consciousness. Neither had anything to do with the actual amount of money they had.

When we live from a place of feeling prosperous, we invoke the laws of giving and receiving. Yet when we live from a place of poverty consciousness, we cut off our supply.

The Law of Circulation

Whether you have a mind-set of prosperity and wealth consciousness, or you fear lack and scarcity, and exist in poverty consciousness, you are living within the law of circulation.

In essence, this law is about giving and receiving. In order to allow the flow of prosperity into your life, you need to understand how your thinking is either allowing, or blocking, the flow of good into your life and business.

Some people I work with, are natural givers. They think nothing of giving of themselves and the things they have to others. They insist on paying for a lunch out with friends. They offer up their time to drive you to the airport. They listen to you tell of your financial difficulties, and they immediately offer you some financial advice or support.

At the other end of the spectrum are the takers. These are the people who are looking to get. They want to receive referrals or obtain money from clients. They are focused on themselves and what they can get out of life. If you are a taker, you think life is for the taking. You see an opportunity and wonder what you can get from it. If you get asked to give a talk, you wonder what's in it for you.

Now, there is no right and wrong to either of these approaches. You may think that being a giver is better than being a taker. However, in order to live and work in the fullest expression of who you are, it's best to be good at both. In essence, you need a balance. If you focus only on either the giving or receiving, soon enough the flow in the other direction starts to dry up.

It is also useful to think about the way you give. If you give with a heavy heart, maybe even feeling resentful about having to give something away, then you are not truly giving. I am not suggesting you need to give all your money, products, or services away for nothing. It is the mind-set of giving that is important. So, when you do give, give with a heart full of love and joy. Don't think about what you will get back in return, just give for the pure joy of giving. Then you will be living from a prosperity mindset.

Maybe you find receiving difficult. You may think there is some sort of catch attached to a gift. You may feel wary of taking it, for then you will feel under some sort of obligation. If you think you are comfortable receiving, ask yourself whether you have a limit on how much you will receive. Maybe you will happily accept someone buying you a drink, a bottle of perfume or a book, but what if someone offered you a holiday, a car, or a house? Would these feel so comfortable to accept?

Think about your life. Do you think you are more of a giver, or more of a taker? Or do you have a good balance? How do you feel about money? Do you feel that you never have enough, no matter how much you earn? Maybe you could journal about what prosperity means to you and see what comes up as you write.

You know you have a good balance when life seems to take care of you. When what you need shows up, when you need it, and you live and work from a mind-set of prosperity.

What are you Really Expecting?

All these things are really important in building a prosperous business. You must allow prosperity consciousness to flow within you if you want to experience it within your business. I'd like you to take this one step further and ask you to call to mind your intentions, and what you believe your outcome will be.

There are three steps in moving from what we want, to experiencing it.

8 Ways to Mind Your Own Business

1. You start off with an idea of what you want to have happen

2. You begin to believe what you want will happen

3. You move to feeling an expectancy and knowingness that it will happen

Each of these three stages has a different mindset.

Let's look at the first one of those... what you want to happen. When you want something to happen, like acquiring external financing to help your new business grow, you could be hoping for the additional cash injection, yet feeling the reality of not having it in this moment. Even though you want the financing, your thoughts, feelings, and experiences are about not with having the financing. Instead of feeling joy in anticipation of the money that is to come, your mood can fluctuate between the high of wanting, and the low of not having it. If you're honest with yourself, you're not entirely sure it will turn up at all. You just hope it will.

When you are living and working from this place, life can feel difficult. It can feel like you are trying to swim upstream against a strong current. This can lead to frustration and irritation of your current situation. You are emotionally experiencing life, with a sense of lack. It is easy to think that what you want will never show up. So, when the going becomes too challenging, you just give up.

When you make the shift to the second way of thinking, believing that the financing will be given, you are starting to move your mind-set into a more positively expectant position. You are saying, even though you are in a place of not having the financing, you are as frustrated about the situation, because you are now prepared to believe that the money you want will show up.

What you may get caught up doing though, is spending time focusing your attention on trying to work out 'how' it will happen. You may even try to plan and orchestrate the path along which you think the money will come to you.

Even though your belief levels are higher, there is still an element of focus on the lack and scarcity of the situation, because you are trying to get the money to come to you, rather than allowing it to come to you in the right way.

Trying to get, allows the element of worry and concern to creep in. When I talk about allowing, it doesn't mean you sit back and do nothing. It means you take inspired action. Instead of trying to force the situation, you let go of the struggle, and just trust. For the money may come to you in a different way than expected.

The last, and definitely the strongest, of the three phases is expectancy. This is where you have a deep seated knowing, that a way to resolve your current situation will be made. You might not know how, but you know it will. When you feel this way, there is no room for doubt or worry. Even when challenges turn up, or one lending institution after another closes its doors to you, there is something within you that knows, a way will be made. Somehow the financing you need will show up.

This is a powerful place to be. When you truly know, and live and work from a place of expectation, it is as though you are experiencing having what you want even before you have it. You talk, act, and behave in a way as though what you want has already been achieved. In this case you already have the financing you want to build your business. You have moved your thinking out from the weeds of the 'how' and instead are looking towards the end result. In this way, you are open and receptive to allowing the financing to come to you though numerous routes, instead of just thinking it will come to you through one route, like a bank.

To create the shift from wanting, to believing, to expecting, you become more discerning about the choice of language you use, as well as the images you create in your mind. In each and every moment, you can choose your thoughts. When you don't practice taking conscious control of your thinking, your thoughts will follow old patterns of behaviour. If you have previously created the habit of seeing only what could go wrong, then this pattern will continue until you decide to change it.

You can raise your belief through the self-talk you use, and the words you speak to others. If you want something, like financing, you must support the belief it will come. If your internal dialogue and the words you speak are in opposition with what you want, for example, if you're filled with doubts and worries, then you are not supporting your ability to believe it can happen.

Many years ago, when my now husband and I bought our home, we took out a twenty-year mortgage, with the first five years having a fixed interest rate. We put nearly all our money into purchasing the house, and I knew as soon as we signed the mortgage offer that I wanted to pay the full loan off when the five-year fixed rate came to an end.

A year after we moved in my partner and I decided to get married. I was putting money aside monthly to pay off the full mortgage, but now we were also saving for our wedding and honeymoon. Within a few months of the wedding I was pregnant and took fourteen months maternity leave from work, many of these months with no pay. Even with all this additional expenditure going out, and reduced income coming in, I still held to the expectation that we would pay the mortgage off at the end of the fixed rate period. I had no idea how it would happen; I just knew in my heart it would.

When we were within twelve months of the end of the fixed rate, I looked at our savings. I knew we had a good amount set aside, but if we continued to save in the same way we would likely have a shortfall at the end of the fixed rate. Yet still there was a deep knowing within me that we would do it. I held on to the feeling, letting go of needing to know how it would happen. Then suddenly, a whole string of additional work opportunities came about, which brought in the exact amount of additional income we needed, just at the right time.

Even though there were times when I couldn't see how we would get enough money, I didn't lose the expectancy and knowing that I felt. The day the five-year fixed term finished, I rang the mortgage lender and paid off the whole mortgage.

Amazing things can happen when you raise your level of thinking from wanting, to believing, and then to expectancy. All it takes is understanding your inner dialogue and then changing anything which isn't in alignment with your highest good, and the highest good of all concerned. All it takes is patience and practice. If I can do it, you can do it too.

If, however, things don't go as planned, like a loan isn't approved, an investor pulls out, or a debtor doesn't pay an invoice on time. Release any need to go into panic mode, being in the state of worry or fear always makes finding a solution more difficult. So, take a deep breath. Affirm that you know the right next steps will reveal themselves to you at the right time. Journal on the situation, using your writing to release any frustration, anger, and irritation, so your emotions become more balanced. Meditate and contemplate on a way forward. Trust and know that the right way will become known to you. Use your imagination to see the situation as you want it to be. As soon as you feel inspired to take action, take it.

Gratitude

One of the greatest practices you can do is one of gratitude. To feel grateful for what is yet to come, is a mark of trust that it will appear.

It is so easy to place our attention on what we don't have and forget what we do.

All through the process of saving the money to pay off my mortgage I kept a feeling of expectancy, as well as a feeling of appreciation and gratitude. At times I could feel myself starting to doubt it would happen, so I looked within and concentrated on the joyful feeling I would have the day I paid it off. As that warm feeling spread throughout me, all I could do was to give thanks. The feeling of gratitude seemed to outpour from me. When you do this, you'll feel a really strong emotion, it can even bring tears to your eyes.

You can express gratitude in different ways. Yes, it can be the strong emotion I described, but it can show up in everyday ways too.

Think about the creditors you pay both personally and for your business. Taking, for example, your utility costs. When you receive a request for payment, you have likely already received the service ahead of payment. You have used the gas or electricity on promise you will pay. The utilities companies trust that you have the financial resources to settle your account.

If you have the automatic tendency to feel your heart drop as a bill arrives, or allow yourself to feel any negative emotion, like fear, concern, or worry about paying, instead turn your thoughts to gratitude. Feel grateful for having received the service in advance. Feel grateful for their trust in your ability to pay. Feel grateful for the financial prosperity you already have. Gather the feelings of gratitude as you make the payment.

Extend that gratitude for all the other things you have in your life. Feel grateful for the support, the love, the resources, the opportunities, and whatever else you have. It is all too easy to see what you don't want and forget what you do. As you learnt earlier, what you focus on, is what will show up. When you focus on giving kindness, kindness will show up for you. When you focus on respecting others, people will respect you. What you give out returns to you. When you give with gratitude, what is returned to you comes with gratitude.

Feel grateful for the prosperity in your life and business, no matter how much or little you have.

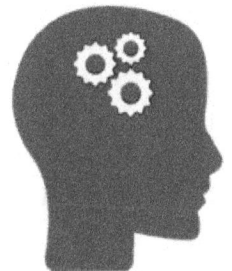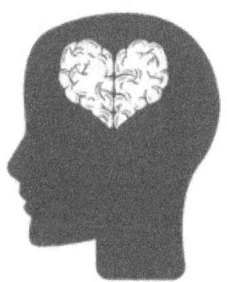

6ᵗʰ Way

8 Ways to Mind Your Own Business

Connection MATTERS

Now this is another one of my favorite topics! Connecting with people is one of my superpowers, I suppose because it is related to communication, a first love for many writers.

Even if you are an introvert, getting revenue is a matter of connecting to potential customers. You will need to develop a level of comfort with it or hire someone to do it for you.

How you connect with potential customers can be categorized into two groups, the online world, and the offline world. While equally important, HOW you connect with these two groups of people will be very different. Of course, there is crossover that will happen naturally, from the offline world to the online world, but it is important to understand the strategy for connecting with them is different.

Now, I have never been uncomfortable in front of a crowd, probably because I sang in the choir and performed solo much of my life. I also won a contest as a teenager, in part by creating and giving several lessons to a small group. I had no idea most people are terrified to speak in front of a group.

When I was in college, one of my summer classes at the University of Alaska was a speech class. We had a wonderful teacher; she was retired but continued teaching summer semester for her own personal enjoyment.

I loved the class; it combined my love of writing with the opportunity to educate others on a topic. It seemed however, everyone else in the class was petrified at the idea of speaking in front of the group, even though summer classes were quite small.

The students worked diligently during the semester to create an engaging speech, and worried continuously about the presentation day. I tried to alleviate some of their fears and worked with a few on their topics, as is my natural tendency.

Our instructor encouraged each sweating and shaking student, with kind words, as they gave their first speech. By the end of the semester, most of my classmates could give a short presentation without looking like they wanted to throw up. None of them ever relished the idea of public speaking quite like I did, but they had become proficient.

It was during speech class, all those years ago, I realized the value of effective communication. Anyone who ever wanted to succeed, would need to master the basics of it. While most of those students would never need to give another formal speech, many of them would benefit from the ability to stand in front of a group and say a few words.

8 Ways to Mind Your Own Business

As a business owner, you also will need to master the basics of effective communication, since you will need to network to get exposure for your new business.

Offline Connections

All around your community you will find opportunities to get together with other business owners and professionals, who gather to network. Usually they offer a couple of minutes for each person to share who they are and talk about what their business does. This is networking.

Only you know what your level of comfort is, when it comes to speaking in front of a group. If the idea of standing to introduce yourself, and your business, is terrifying, you will want to work on this ahead of time.

Having worked with new business owners and authors for so many years, I have developed a simple formula to remove some of the stress of the networking introduction. Fill in the blanks and practice, practice, practice the paragraph.

Hello, I'm (fill in this blank) with (the name of your company). I work with (fill in the blank with WHO you work with) who want to (what benefit do you offer them) to (why do they want the benefit).

Here is an example from my own business.

"Hello, I'm Clara Rose with Intentional Influence. I work with entrepreneurs and professionals, who want to write, speak, and lead, to expand their influence and generate more leads."

Simple, I state who I am and the name of my company, who I work with, and the benefits I bring to them.

Once you have memorized your basic introduction, in time as your confidence grows, you will be able to change it up or expand on it. If you continue to struggle, find a local Toast Masters group to join or hire a coach help you. This is so important, don't leave it to chance, but don't let it be an excuse to NOT get out there.

Check with local business associations and your chamber of commerce, for the best places to network. Finding a place to network shouldn't be a problem, in fact, you can network so much that you never get any work done.

If you are an extrovert, be careful to not confuse networking with income producing activity. It should only consume about twenty percent of your time.

Effective networking is about building relationships, you can't just show up and expect it to lead to business growth. It takes time to nurture and build those relationships, so show up before the meeting and spend time with people. Stay after the meeting to connect with others who hang around.

If you really want to take advantage of those networking opportunities, schedule a follow up time for coffee or lunch with someone you met. Get to know them and their business. The resulting relationship will organically lead to business and referrals.

We make local connections when we network, but it can be a balancing act. Your time is valuable, take care that you spend it wisely.

Online Connections

It is easier than ever to connect with potential customers online. The number of platforms designed to connect us, grows almost daily, it can be overwhelming to try and keep up. I am not suggesting you should even try. New platforms launch, current platforms change, and old platforms fade away, faster than you can imagine. Even if you had a team dedicated to growing your presence on ALL the social media platforms available, it is not possible.

During your original due diligence, when you started this new journey, you should have discovered where your ideal customer was hanging out online. If you skipped that step, now is the time to go back and do it. It is important to know where they are, so your marketing efforts are effective.

If your products or services are geared toward the consumer instead of another business, it means you will find your customers where you find consumers. Consider Facebook or Pinterest to connect with them. If you serve businesses, look for places that professionals and business owners hang out, like LinkedIn. Simple, right?!?

Start with two or three online platforms where your ideal customers are. If that is overwhelming to you, start with just one. As you master each platform, you can add another one. Keep in mind, this is not an income producing activity, and needs to stick to the twenty percent rule about spending your time.

While the digital connections we make are not the same as face to face interactions, they can be just as viable business connections. In fact, they can be easier to nurture since some of it can be automated, but be careful, social media is NOT a set it and forget it endeavour, it is intended to be social in nature. That means we must interact for it to be effective. This is done best with authenticity and transparency.

Consistency is the key to cutting through the noise of social media. If you only show up occasionally, the noise of thousands of other people will make it impossible to hear your message. I like to tell my clients, "Show up, speak up, and make a difference." In other words, you need to be seen, have something to say, and to contribute. To accomplish this, automation is sometimes necessary. After all, we have lives to live and a business to run. Automation is all about the tools.

If you follow me on social media, you have heard or seen me say, "Success is a matter of influence, but influence is NOT accidental. It comes from the implementation of a sound strategy, with the correct resources and tools."

8 Ways to Mind Your Own Business

It's a bit of a mantra for me. It reminds me, and my followers, that success will come as a result of having a strategy which includes resources and tools, to make my work easier.

Just like social media platforms, resources and tools change often. I am always on the lookout for the next great tool, to help me work smarter instead of harder. That's not to say I jump ship every time a new tool comes along. Shiny object syndrome can be a real time waster. It does mean I pay attention to new features that might be more beneficial to my productivity.

Finding a tool to automate some of your social media posting is essential. There is controversy about the automated posts not getting the same ranking as live posts. If you are concerned, you can schedule posts within the platform, just set aside some time and schedule them in bulk. No one has the time to sit at the computer all day posting. If you do, you are probably not making any money in your business. The time you spend on social media should be time spent socializing and connecting, so you can build relationships, that will organically lead to referrals and business.

To build trust and relationship in the online environment, we need to show that we are real people, with real lives. Real people have families, pets, beliefs, birthdays, hopes, and dreams. They laugh at jokes, express how they feel about things, and they comment on conversations around them. Social media makes it easy to do this digitally.

When others can see and feel the heart behind your marketing message online, it gives them the opportunity to self-identify as belonging to your tribe... because they are like you. These people are the mostly likely to become your raving fans and customers.

The ability to connect with potential customers or clients, will make your success possible. After all, they are the source of revenue for your new business. Everything hinges on reaching them, connecting with them, and convincing them that YOUR product or service is the answer to their wants or needs.

8 Ways to Mind Your Own Business

Inspired Connection

The greatest and most wonderful connection we can ever make is the one with ourselves. Knowing yourself at a deeper level is one of the most wonderful gifts you can give yourself, but how many of us actually make that journey? Very few.

We live in a society where it is easy to distract ourselves from our problems. When faced with difficult economic times, there are certain businesses, like the entertainment industry, which flourish. This is because we use entertainment as a distraction.

We are afraid to get to know ourselves for fear of what might be lurking inside. Yet how can we make deep and meaningful relationships with others, if we are not able to have one with our-self?

In building your business you'll likely want to influence others. An influencer is a great communicator, who shares knowledge, compassion, and vulnerability. So, on your journey of making inspired connections, the first connection to make is the one with yourself.

Connecting with the Wonderfulness that is YOU

I would like to ask you to be honest with yourself. How well do you really know you? You may reply, of course I know me, I'm ME. Who else is going to know me better than ME?

How often do you stop and check-in with yourself? Do you meditate and journal daily, enjoying time alone with yourself and the silence within? Do you listen to, and take action, on your intuition? Do you regularly check-in with how your body feels? If you get a headache or a small level of discomfort, do you stop and check in with your body to find out what has caused this discomfort? Or do you immediately pop a pain killer and carry on regardless?

Far too often the latter approach is taken. We continue to push our minds and our bodies through pain and discomfort, popping pills to deal with the symptom, without searching for the cause.

It is easy to live in our heads, to think our body is just a vehicle to carry us around. In doing this, we fail to fully connect with our body, and it is only when a major illness or injury occurs, that we stop and see what our disconnection has led to. Then, we are potentially faced with a difficult journey back to health.

If only, we think, we hadn't kept pushing ourselves to work that punishing twelve-hour day. If only we hadn't ignored those headaches… stomach cramps… back twinges. If only…

8 Ways to Mind Your Own Business

It is never too late to begin connecting with yourself again. Start your journey with a meditation each day. There is no right or wrong way to meditate. Find a comfortable seated position where you can safely close your eyes and place your awareness on your breath.

Maybe you'll want to focus on the rise and fall of your tummy, or even on the feeling of air coming in and out of your nostrils. Thoughts will undoubtedly pop into your mind, and when they do, acknowledge them, and allow them to float away without getting caught up in them. If you do find yourself getting caught up in them, lovingly bring yourself back to focusing on your breath.

This is a wonderful way to begin reconnecting with yourself. You can extend this by allowing yourself a period of silence every day. Instead of filling every quiet moment with sound, enjoy the silence.

If you are in the car turn off the radio and drive in silence, listening to the natural sounds around you. If you are walking with someone, know that you don't have to fill every empty second with conversation. Know that it is nourishing to have a bit of space between words.

If this is difficult for you, and I have certainly had clients who found this difficult, start slowly. Tell yourself safety and knowledge can be found in silence. It is safe to know yourself. The silence will help you to appreciate yourself more. It will give you the time and space to know what next step feels right for you, rather than doing something for the sake of it.

Finally, tune into your body. It is a gold mine of information which we don't often tap into. Before I started on this spiritually inspired, personal development journey, I lived much more in my head. If I felt a twinge, I took a pain killer. I didn't stop to listen to my body. It was as if I thought my body was just a mechanical device to carry around my mind.

I smile as I think of that now.

Yet, when I started to connect with me, I found out so much more about myself. I learnt how far I could push myself. When I needed to rest. How a pain could tell me there was a trapped emotion being held, which when released the pain would naturally go.

This doesn't mean I won't need to seek medical advice at times, however, when I listen to what my body is telling me, I can often make small adjustments, and allow my body to regain its normal and natural healthy balance.

So, dare to make that connection with you. Listen to what your body needs. Listen for the spark of inspiration that will carry you forward. Refresh and rejuvenate yourself by listening to the silence.

The better you know yourself, the better connections you will be able to create with others. For you will be offering them something they can relate to.

8 Ways to Mind Your Own Business

Release the Need to Please Others

Finding and building your tribe can feel daunting when you are first starting out. It is easy to fall into the trap of being who you think you should be in order to connect with others. But don't. Dare to be true to you.

As an entrepreneur creating a new business, it is easy to get into the head space of thinking you need to tailor who you are, and what you offer, in order to be acceptable to other people. This is different than looking at the market, identifying a need, and filling it, which is a good idea. Instead, I am talking about doing, acting, behaving, or being, in a way you think is acceptable to other people, so they will approve of you.

We all have different expectations about how people should act or behave. When we live our life trying to meet the expectations of others, we are not living our own truths. We are essentially saying, I will only be happy if others approve of me. You are giving others control over your happiness.

When I was employed by a firm, I found myself acting in a way to please my employers. I adopted certain styles of body language to convey that I was interested in a conversation, when deep down I wasn't really. When I wanted a promotion, I would tailor my language and say things I knew those recruiting would want to hear. I became a carbon copy of what they wanted as an employee… whilst inside I felt like I was slowly dying.

I was acting in order for my boss to be happy, so I could gain his approval. If he approved of me, I would be happy. Otherwise I wasn't. So, my happiness rested entirely on another person.

What a silly thing to do!

Now reflect on you, and what you want from your new business. If you are wanting to build a tribe of loyal and engaged followers, don't tailor yourself to try and please them and seek their approval. That won't work, you can never please everyone. Instead, follow your truth and speak your word. Dare to follow your heart and allow your actions and behaviours to come from this place.

The people who are interested in what you have to say and what your business offers, will find you. They will love you because you speak from an authentic place, where you are true to you. Because you dare to shine your light, you give them permission to shine theirs too... to step into their greatness.

So, release any need within you to please others. Instead come from a whole-hearted place of pleasing yourself and speaking your truth.

Sharing your Voice

When you know who you are and release the need to BE any certain way to please others, you will build inspired connections with others, from your place of truth.

8 Ways to Mind Your Own Business

Clara beautifully described making both face to face and online connections in the previous chapter. She mentioned speaking came easily for her, but you may either feel comfortable or uncomfortable speaking in public. I had a different experience of public speaking, for I have felt both comfortable and painfully shy speaking in front of others.

After my dad died, three weeks after my fifteenth birthday, my self-esteem and confidence shot through the floor. I had always been shy as a young child, but now my levels of deserving and worthiness were below floor level. They remained stuck like that for several years, until the age of around nineteen when I was introduced to self-help books. They weren't my books, my partner was forced to buy them through a company he was working for, but neither of us was reading them. Then one day, I looked at the stack of books and I started thumbing through them.

Over the next few years, I became a closet reader of personal development material, but I kept the books hidden and didn't tell anyone, for fear they would think I was nuts. In time the books slowly helped me to raise my confidence and self-esteem.

In my early twenties when I was working in finance, I remember one painful moment, sitting with a group around a large conference table, and we were all asked to introduce ourselves.

It was just a case of saying my name, job role and department, yet the thought of doing this terrified me. I could feel my legs shake under the table. As the introductions were being made, all I could think about was what I was going to say. I couldn't focus on anyone else. When it got to my turn, the words came out in a garbled rush. If you feel like that, know that you aren't alone.

A year later when I was watching the film, Robin Hood Prince of Thieves, I remember thinking… I could act like that. As soon as I thought it, something inside me clicked. Suddenly I was off searching for amateur dramatic groups in my area. I was terrified and excited all at the same time.

I went along to a group and found my stage fright held me back. The people there were lovely, and soon I was acting in a short play. I got cast in another play, then another, taking bigger and bigger roles. Then a different theatre company had a member of their cast walk out two weeks before curtain up. I was asked if I'd save the show and step in. I did it, and it was wonderful.

The main city Theatre Royal held auditions for a production of Threepenny Opera, I went along and was cast in a major role. I did a further two shows with them, in their smaller theatre to start with, but the last show was on their main stage, running for two whole weeks in front of around twelve hundred people a performance.

Now I feel completely comfortable in front of an audience. But it took courage, practice, and shifting my belief in myself to do it.

8 Ways to Mind Your Own Business

Two of the ways which helped me to turn my confidence around was the language I used, and the mind movies I played.

Say you are about to attend a networking event. What are your thoughts about it? What are you saying to yourself? What mental images are you creating? Are you using words and images that scare you? If you are feeling worried about attending, you probably are scaring yourself. Know you have the power to change this.

As you make your way to the networking event, think about the words you are thinking, and how you are feeling. Tell yourself you are a good communicator. That you make connections easily and effortlessly, and the right words always come to you. Then see yourself in your mind's eye talking to people confidently, and with ease. Really feel the feelings of this playing out in your mind.

Your mind doesn't know the difference between what is happening in reality, and what is vividly imagined. If you can spend time vividly imagining what a successful networking event looks and feels like for you, you will find this will transfer into your reality.

The Power of Story

When I am making connections, both in person and online, the one thing I find helpful is the use of the power of story. Our brains are hardwired for story. It is the way humans have learnt about themselves and the world around them, going back thousands of years. Before humans had written communication, they passed on legends and traditions through story telling.

Even as a young child my parents read stories to me. I did the same with my daughter. It helps us to understand the world around us and how we fit into it.

I have found in some communication situations, like networking, that everyone uses the same introduction formula. They start with their name and what they do. For example, if a woman stands up and introduces herself as a painter and decorator, in my mind I think, I don't need a painter and decorator, so I switch off from fully listening. Had she taken a different tack and started with a story about how her work transforms lives, and yes, anything we do can have a transformative effect on someone's life, then her words would have been more engaging.

Let me explain. I don't get up and say, "Hi, I'm Debbie Clement-Large and I'm a Life & Leadership Coach and founder of the award winning Why follow the Herd coaching practice." Because those who think they don't want the services of a coach will stop listening. Yet in my experience, what we want and what we need are often two different things. In order to help them to remain open to listening, I introduce myself in a different way.

I might say, "Imagine you're a beautiful oak tree set in a gorgeous landscape. You want to be seen at your best, so you pay attention to pruning and shaping your branches, and shining your leaves, so everyone will see how wonderful you look. Your branches and leaves represent your actions, behaviours and the words you use to others. These are all external things. Yet, in order to grow and become resilient, a tree will obtain its nutrients through its roots. Your root system is your self-esteem and confidence. If you focus entirely on your outside appearance, to the detriment of building a big strong root system, then when a big storm comes along, it could send you crashing to the floor. If you want to learn how to build your inner resilience and strengthen your roots, talk to me… I'm Debbie Clement-Large, a Life & Leadership Coach, and founder of the award winning Why follow the Herd coaching practice."

Notice I leave introducing myself until the end, when they are fully engaged, having listened to the story.

There really is no right or wrong way to communicate who you are and what you do with other people, the trick is to find a way that is comfortable for you. So, dare to explore different ways and see which works best for you. I know I get a lot of people remembering me long after a networking event, which, of course, is what I am after.

The same goes for communicating online too. Try not to only give the facts about your product or service but think about how you can weave it into a story. Maybe a story of how you have made a difference to yourself or a client.

Remember, what people want is not what always what they need. Where they may initially think that they don't want your services, after listening to you, or reading your blog, they may find they do actually need them.

Enjoy being creative with your communication. Dare to be you! Your tribe will appreciate and love your authenticity. Remember that great communicating starts with knowing yourself. So, take time out for a bit of quiet each day, and reconnect with you and listen to your intuition.

If the thought of speaking in public feels scary, do what Clara suggested and join Toastmasters, or do what I did and join a theatre group. Either way it is all about building confidence and belief in yourself and getting out there.

Lastly, support your journey with nourishing self-talk. Always be gentle and loving with yourself, even if you think you've messed up. It is all a learning journey.

Most importantly, have fun.

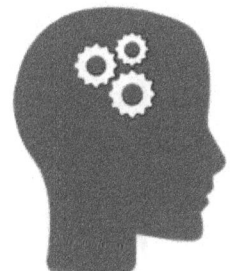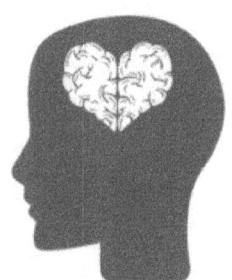

7th Way

Customer MATTERS

Success in your new business is a matter of attracting customers, who buy your products or services. No customers, no business. It sounds simplistic but everything hinges on a steady flow of customers bringing in revenue, so your business will thrive.

Attracting new customers will always be important and finding ways to stand out from the crowd will definitely help. Being unique or offering more value for a similar price is a staple for any business, new or established, but to really thrive you must offer more. More than just a sale, it's essential to offer a great customer experience.

These days, when you hear someone talking about a customer or a user experience, they are typically talking about a digital software or website. I am talking about something else.

Think about the customer journey again, we discussed it in a previous chapter. As you walk through the experience of being a customer in your own business… take note of how you FEEL. Pay attention to the human element and interactions that take place during the customer's time with your business.

Yes, you want to find out if the process of working with your company was easy or complicated; but just as important, did you feel valued as a customer? Did it feel cold and driven by a money transaction, or did you feel appreciated and served?

Serve

If I could only differentiate my business in one way, I would pick service. Perhaps it is easier because I sell services instead of products, for the most part. I truly feel like I am being of service to my clients, helping them build more influence and generate more leads.

For instance, when one of my clients finishes writing their book and we are ready to publish, I have helped them through a ton of work. Together we created their content, edited, and formatted their manuscript, and pulled it all together for print. During the hours and hours of creative collaboration, I served them.

When one of my client's steps onto a stage for their first speaking engagement, or launches their new movement or podcast, I am like a parent bursting with pride. I pour knowledge into them, and they achieved a goal or dream. I served them.

I want them to FEEL like I have been an invaluable part of the process… that I was of service to them. Together, we created something they had only dreamed of doing, or had been trying

8 Ways to Mind Your Own Business

to do alone for years. For me, it's one of the joys of my business, it leaves me feeling fulfilled.

You will never know how your product or service impacted your customers unless you ask them. I recommend you make it a practice to ask for customer feedback, you will be amazed by what you learn.

Pay attention to praises, they tell you what you are doing right, and pay even more attention to the negative comments. Don't dwell on the negatives but learn and grow from them. Perhaps you can fix a problem for a customer and save the relationship. When you care enough to address an issue, you are showing them they matter. I can think of more than one occasion where this effort has retained a client, and even created a fan.

As a business owner, it should be your goal to meet the needs of your customers. Consider all the ways you can serve them. If you are selling a product instead of a service, serving them might come in the form of education about your products. Or it might be the time you take, helping them make a buying decision. I call it customer service, and it's just good business.

Integrity

The word integrity is often used in marketing materials, added to vision or mission statements, and even used in company taglines. If a company values integrity and has made it a part of their culture, it is a powerful marketing tool.

Using the word integrity, promises that you as a business owner, will do the right thing for your employees and customers, always. Integrity means you stand behind your products or services, and fix things, should something go wrong.

Even when no one is looking, integrity means you will do the right thing.

Be sure to manage customer expectations during each step of the customer journey with your company. This will help eliminate some of the potential misunderstandings that can lead to unhappy customers. A well-informed customer is more likely to have a positive feeling about their decision to work with you. The larger the purchase price, the better the education process needs to be.

Have a written plan in place for handling customer disputes and complaints. A good plan creates a consistent means for resolution, instead of a knee jerk reaction when something happens. This will more than likely be one of the policies and procedures you created during the chapter on operation matters. If not, this is a good time to add it.

Sadly, these days there seems to be an abundance of scammers that leave us all feeling guarded during business dealings. These individuals clearly have no integrity. They have no regard for the damage they might cause, they only care about filling their pockets with money they did not earn.

While I can only say, "Shame on them for being terrible human beings," they do make it easy for us to stand out. We simply need to offer quality products or services, great customer service, and always do what we say we will. Pretty easy right?!?

Gratitude

There is an abundance of studies, trainings, and books available on the topic of gratitude, and the value it brings to a business. In fact, gratitude brings value to every part of our lives, but today we are focusing on your new business.

Customers want to feel they are spending their money well. More and more, they want to know the companies they do business with, and support with their dollars, care about the community around them.

It's not enough to just tell your customers that you care, it can seem hollow and less than authentic if they can't see HOW you care. Finding ways to give back to your local community is a great start for showing, instead of telling, that you care.

It doesn't need to cost you a ton of money either, you can create a shared opportunity to serve in your community. There is never a shortage of worthy social causes and local projects to rally around. Find something that resonates with you and your ideal customers, and send out a rally cry, "Join us as we make a difference." Serving together creates an emotional connection that is the base of a tribe mentality, encouraging them to self-identify as part of your family.

If you really want to embrace a culture of gratitude and caring, find a cause that resonates deeply with you and become a champion of the cause. Like minded customers will join you, and as an added benefit, you will make a difference in your community.

Customers also want to feel appreciated for their loyalty. Consider how you might create a loyalty or reward program for your customers. They will love the rewards or savings you offer, and you can express gratitude and appreciation in a tangible way.

Your company is still new but start planning now for a future customer appreciation event. It can be a few hours on a Saturday afternoon, or a month of celebration. You can even have a virtual event on social media instead of a live event. As long as you are offering some fun and savings, you will make your customers feel like a valued member of the family.

If you have the ability to personalize your products or services, you have gratitude gold. It says to your customer, "We see that you are unique, and we honor it." Nothing builds a connection faster than using your customer's name. Even something as simple as a personalized note or thank you card can create a fan.

Expressions of gratitude need to be sprinkled throughout the customer's journey with your company. A sincere welcome can say, "We're glad you are here, and you matter to us." The potential ideas for showing gratitude are endless, and so are the benefits. Gratitude Matters.

In fact, it is so important, it's never too soon to start showing it. It is easier than ever to connect with potential customers, thanks to social media, and this is often the start of your customer's journey with you. It is the perfect time to demonstrate an attitude of appreciation AND a culture of caring.

The bottom line is this, if you find ways to make a difference, and show appreciation for your customers, you will create long term sustainability for your new company. By building a culture of caring, you can authentically show appreciation for those people who make your success possible.

Your customers are your most valuable assets. When you take the time to make them feel like they matter, you create raving fans.

8 Ways to Mind Your Own Business

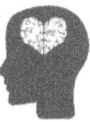

Inspired Customer

As an inspired entrepreneur you will want to inspire your customers. You will want them to connect with you, to become interested in what you have to offer, to purchase goods and services from you, to become a loyal repeat customer, and a raving fan of your goods and services. In essence you'll want your business to inspire others to take action.

Wherever you are starting from, know this is possible. You may already have an established customer list, or you may just be starting out, in either case know that even through the noise of advertising and social media, you will be able to connect with your audience… your tribe.

Success Intelligence

Some of your most valuable tools, as you build and nurture your tribe, is the language you use, and the mind movies you create.

I have already mentioned the importance of the language you use and being true to yourself. These things are so important, they are worth mentioning again.

Know your mailing list is your best asset. Yes, it is good to have a lot of followers on social media, but until they have converted to your list, it may only take an algorithm or policy change on the social media site, for your followers to disappear.

I have found building my list to be an interesting experience. It has brought me through a different array of emotions, from the joy of having new people sign up, to wondering why they won't sign up. I have concerned myself with what others will think of my content, and whether people want to read what I'm writing.

I found myself reaching for my toolbox of tools when I experienced these different emotions.

It is always good to acknowledge these emotions, for we can learn so much from them. If you are feeling concerned about what other people think of your content, pay attention to why that is bothering you. If you are feeling frustrated at the lack of opt-ins, ask yourself why numbers matter, and why you feel as you do. These are wonderful indicators of your beliefs. I always find when I journal on these thoughts and emotions, I discover a lot about myself I hadn't really realised. This kind of thinking shows me my insecurities, which I can then work on.

What other people think about us is none of our business. Their thoughts are their business. Yet, I know how much we can take on the opinions of others and make them our own.

8 Ways to Mind Your Own Business

Think about how you feel about both your current customers, and your future customers. Are you taking your current customers for granted? Are you only focused on gaining more? Are you lovingly appreciating those who open your emails? My average weekly click open rate is 35%. I feel blessed in the sheer quantity of emails and marketing that drop into everyone's inboxes, that so many are sharing their precious time with me. I feel blessed for this opportunity to be of service. It really is special.

I would like to share with you my success secrets. Firstly, be consciously aware of your language. Are your thoughts focused on what you don't have, for instance, the lack of numbers on your list? Or what you do have, like those who already open your mailings? Steer your language away from wanting to get and focus on how you can give and be of service. Know that life is lining you up with the right people. It is better to have smaller and highly engaged list, than a larger colder mailing list.

Be clear on what you want. Focus your attention on it. If you have any thinking to the contrary, remove it. Do not even allow yourself to think of lack and limitation. Talk yourself up into a place of knowingness and expectation, and then be patient. Life unfolds in perfect timing. Release any need to have the world the way you want it to be, and instead allow.

To make this change say words like, *I am a wonderful attractor of new ways to be of service in my business*. Words are just words unless we believe them. Feel the energetic power behind the words. Say them over and over. If you feel they are a lie or notice there is some form of inner discomfort as you say them, great, you are discovering a place of resistance within you which you can work on.

If you experience resistance, either meditate on the feeling, or journal about it. See what comes up for you. It is only in doing this kind of work that you will be able to start breaking through any barriers which are holding you back from the success you want.

Words and feelings are powerful, but our imagination has even more power. When I spend time with my clients, I find this is an underused tool. Or at least it is in the direction of the things they want. What they can be incredibly good at, is using their imagination to scare themselves.

A small incident can suddenly snowball into something major within a very short time in our minds, if our thinking is left unchecked. When I was employed, I had to go through numerous work restructures. These were frequent and always with the intention of saving money, so job cuts were a common feature. Over time I found myself creating negative inner dialogue and mind movies when the mention of a new restructure was made. Immediately my heart would sink, I would think about the awfulness of having to reapply for my job. My inner dialogue was full of competition and struggle. My mind would create movies of losing my job, and what would happen once the money stopped.

I was creating the language and mind movies of fear and doom, when in reality the only thing that had happened was, I had been informed of a restructure. I was scaring myself with my thoughts and my imagination.

What changes can you commit to, in order to feel a greater inspired connection to your customers, both current and future? What can you learn from your current thoughts, actions, and behaviours? Know what you want and speak the words which support it. Feel the feelings of the words and see the vision of interacting with customers the way you want it to be.

Re-Writing the Past

You can take the use of your imagination one step further. Instead of using it to create an image of what you want to happen, you can use it to re-frame what has happened in the past. This is a great way to let go of old unwanted emotions.

Say you had a bad experience dealing with a client. Maybe you felt they were being unreasonable, and you became irritated or annoyed with them. Maybe they became angry with you and talked to you in a way which was dis-respectful and hurtful. When we experience something like this, it can be easy to re-play the event over and over in our minds. We can even go over all the things we could have said, or we wished we would have said, or even what we wished we hadn't said! This can go on for days, weeks, and potentially even longer. When we do this, it causes us suffering.

So, I would like to invite you to use your imagination to change the event, and thereby reduce the energy attachment you have to it. Your subconscious doesn't know the difference between something which is actually happening, and a vividly imaged experience. Take some time to sit quietly, I suggest you spend a few moments concentrating on your breath. Allow your awareness to focus on the rise and fall of your belly.

When you feel calm and centred, allow your mind to re-create the scene which you'd like to re-frame. As the scene unfolds, know that you can create a new response to what is happening. Realise that you have no control over changing the actions and behaviours of another person, only yourself. As you run through the movie in your mind, deal with the situation in the way you would have wanted to do so. Really feel the feelings of communicating the way you would have wanted to communicate. Release any need to take anything personally. As you replay the situation in your mind, see and feel your reactions to the situation in a way that make you feel good. There is no right or wrong way to do this, if it feels good, that is all you can do.

If you had a strong reaction to the incident, you might like to keep repeating this exercise until you are able to fully change how you feel about it. Alternatively, you can write about it in your journal, both from your perspective, and that of the other person. Doing either of these exercises will help you gain a better understanding of your emotions and reactions, and what you can learn from them. It will also help you to practice forgiveness, for we heal ourselves when we learn to practice the art of letting go. Just know that these exercises work, and there is no right or wrong way of doing them.

The Customer Journey

You may also want to use your imagination to visualise your business from your customer's point of view and help you to create a wonderful experience for your customers. I went through this briefly in an earlier chapter, but it is such a valuable exercise I wanted to repeat it again here.

You can do this exercise multiple times, each time creating a mind movie for a specific way your customers come into contact with you. From joining your mailing list, to purchasing your products or services, to your returns process, or raising questions, or complaints, or any other way you can think of.

Choose one specific channel of communication and then imagine you are a customer going through that particular process. Put yourself in their shoes, and really see and feel what that experience is like for them. Pay attention to anything that doesn't feel good, for this is giving you valuable information on where and how you can change the process.

Gratitude

Gratitude is another really important topic, and one which can easily be overlooked.

At one of my workshops, a participant said that he could have ten things on his to-do list at the start of the day. By the end of the day he had completed nine of the things of his list yet could only focus on the one thing he hadn't accomplished.

When we see and feel lack in this way, we aren't experiencing gratitude. Seeing only lack, comes from the place of ego. No matter how much we do, our ego always wants more. It will never be satisfied. It wants us to accomplish more, to do it faster and better than everyone else. If we listen to it, we never feel good enough.

Gratitude can be used in multiple ways. Being grateful for you, who you are and what you do. Being grateful for customers past, present, and future, and being grateful for all those who support your journey in creating a wonderful business.

How you practice gratitude is unique to you. I practice it in different ways depending on where I am. When I am out walking with my dog in the woods I think, or say out loud, a list of things I am grateful for. I start each sentence with, *I am grateful for...* When I do this, it creates a wonderful lightness in my energy. Even after thinking of only ten things I can feel a difference.

Another method I use is to write down the things I am grateful for. In the same way I say it out loud, I start each sentence with, I am grateful for...

8 Ways to Mind Your Own Business

If you feel a real connection with writing, you will enjoy writing these down.

You can be grateful for the big things, or the small things. I even feel grateful for the air I breathe, knowing there is an endless supply, and that my next breath will be there when I want it. I don't have to fight for it, I can relax and allow. There really is so much to be grateful for.

At different times during the day, stop and think of things to feel thankful for. Maybe when a purchase is made, a booking taken, a product posted, and a bill is paid. Practice it for the small things, like when someone makes you a cup of tea, as well as the big things, like winning a large contract. The more you focus your attention on what you feel grateful for, the more things to feel grateful for, will show up in your life and business.

Release the Need to Get

Lastly, release the need to get. Remember back to an earlier chapter when I talked about the law of circulation… I said that life, and business, works well when we are good at giving and receiving.

Be thankful for all the things you receive in your life and business, as well as the opportunities to be of service. Think more about how you can give. You may want to give some of your products or services away to good causes. You might want to share your financial abundance, or your knowledge and experience, or even tips on building a business that you've learnt along the way. Even providing a friendly ear when someone needs it or making a cuppa for someone is a wonderful way to give. You can be of service in big or small ways. Sometimes what may seem like a small gift, such as a smile, may mean a lot to another person.

As we end this chapter know that customers do matter, and when you inspire them, they become raving fans. Use the power of your inner dialogue, spoken word and mind movies to create the experience you want with your customers, as well as the experience you want them to have with you. Feel grateful for every interaction, and when something doesn't go to plan, think about how you can learn from it. Stick to your word and treat people as you would want to be treated.

The important thing is to work from a place of believing, knowing, and expecting that you already are, and will continue to create, an inspired connection with your customers.

8 Ways to Mind Your Own Business

 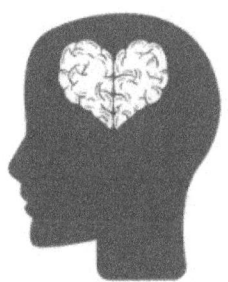

8th Way

Employee MATTERS

There comes a time for each business owner, when they must make a choice. As business grows, even the most strategic and organized owner will reach a point where it is no longer possible to manage alone.

It is a choice. Of course, you can make the decision to only take on an amount of work you can handle by yourself. Easier said than done!

If you are selling a product with automations in place, you won't have much control over the sales or when they will come. If solopreneur is your goal, you will want to plan it from the start, so you can build a business you have more control over.

Most of us start a business hoping it will grow, reaching a point where we can hire some help. A thriving company with more sales, is usually the goal. Growth is exciting, but it also brings some new challenges to your business.

My co-author, Debbie, will cover some of the important mindset and leadership topics, but I want to prepare you with some of the nuts and bolts of employee matters.

Before you jump right on the employee train, consider some of the great options available that offer FREE help to your business. Interns, work study, and apprenticeship programs!

Check with your local college or university to see if they have an intern program. They might have a job board you can utilize, where students check for opportunities. If not, don't worry, you can still place job listings in other places, offering an intern position.

In my husband's business, we have used high school students from the work study program. This gives the student, school credits towards graduation and real-life experience in the workplace. We have always enjoyed the eagerness of these young people, and of course the extra help for free! I paid them in food and goodies, which they appreciated.

Finally, an often-overlooked option, is the apprenticeship program. In the past, most trades were passed on through apprenticeship. When someone entered the workforce, they could learn a trade directly from the master craftsman. While it is not as common these days, there is a move back to this practice.

Apprenticeship might be the perfect addition to your new company. There just might be an apprentice looking to learn from your expertise.

Many people just entering, or reentering, the workforce will jump on the opportunity to learn from you and your business. Have a look at some of these options before settling on a paid position.

Time to Grow

Let's start by discussing what kind of paid help you might be considering. You can hire traditional employees, contract employees, or use a service to meet the needs of your growing business. Each option comes with different governing rules, you will want to understand the ramifications of each before you make your decision.

If you hire traditional employees, they usually work set hours and get a regular paycheck from you. You control their schedule and the day to day activities of their job description. Of course, you also have the added responsibility of regular payroll, employee taxes, and benefits, if you offer them. This is a big step for most new businesses, it can be scary to be financially responsible for other people.

One way to mitigate some of the risk and fear factor, is a trial option. You can find any number of ways to take a test drive with potential employees, but the easiest is with a recruitment company or staffing agency.

Based on your criteria, the agency assumes the time commitment of resumes and interviews and send temporary assignment staff. These folks are paid by the agency and you have no obligation to hire them. Of course, you WILL pay the agency for the staff member, while you have them. This is an easy way to fill a position on a trial basis. If it is NOT a good fit, the agency can send you someone else. If you decide to hire the person, the agency will usually require a fee to release them to you.

Either way, you were able to test out a new person, without the commitment of hiring them.

Brick and mortar businesses, like a local coffee shop, require the traditional employee employer relationship. It is the hardest in my opinion. They are people, with lives outside of your business. They might have a spouse and kids, animals to care for, a church or charity they support, and even another job. If you care about people, you run the risk of getting too involved in their personal lives, and not being as objective about their employment. Be sure you are clear about your expectations and the consequences for noncompliance. Don't misunderstand, I believe a good employer is a strong leader, who cares about people and leads by example, but it's important to maintain a balance. You are their employer first and foremost.

In your business, if you decide contract employees are a better option, you need to understand that they work differently. They work more independently, often on their own schedule and generally work project based. The focus is on the results they produce, not on their day to day activities. In the U.S., contract employees usually get paid on a 1099 basis; that is to say, you will not be holding out taxes for them or paying any portion of their tax liability. Be sure to check the local laws in your area. Sometimes you are not their only employer, and you must be careful to not treat them like a regular employee.

I recommend you have a non-disclosure agreement in place with contract employees, it protects any proprietary information or processes you have. While they can be difficult to enforce, a non-compete agreement will also help protect you from someone learning your trade secrets, and then opening a competing business next door!

I have had both traditional and contract employees, but my favorite way to get help in my business is through a service provider, not direct employment. My business has an ebb and flow to it, so this option allows me to get help when it's required without the ongoing commitment. When I am swamped with clients, I can call one of my favorite service providers, and get the extra help I need.

Service providers come in all sorts of packages. Figure out what services would take the most pressure off you, so you can focus on other things. For me, I outsource the things I don't enjoy… because I can! That's one of the benefits of owning your own business. Bookkeeping, social media marketing, customer care, and scheduling; are all great places to get some help in your growing business. A word of caution; make sure you are hiring a business as your service provider. If not, you are hiring a contract employee and recordkeeping requirements are different.

One big perk to using a service provider versus direct employment, is that a business will offer you more protection against theft. It's sad to say, but the topic needs to be addressed. Over the years, as a business owner, we have had more than one theft of property or intellectual property, and even one embezzlement. Be aware, be smart, and not overly trusting. It is not my natural state, but I have learned to be more cautious!

Alternatively, you can hire a virtual assistant to help with administrative work. They usually offer an hourly rate, or weekly / monthly rate for a set number of hours, but they are a contracted service, not an employee, otherwise there may be tax implications. As a contracted service you can only dictate the outcome of their efforts and deadlines. This is a great way to get some help and free up your time. There are plenty of people online offering VA services, be sure to do your due diligence before contracting with one. Check their references, exchange a few emails, and have a couple of conversations with them, to ensure a good fit. Once you find a good VA, treat them like the gold they are!

If you are only hiring service providers, your due diligence is different. I like to start by stalking them on social media! Well, not really stalking them, but you can learn a lot about people on their social media profiles and business pages. Take some time and look at the people they associate with; remember that saying, "You are a combination of the people you hang out with." It's a saying for a reason!

My clients are valuable to me, I am careful who I expose them too. When I work with a service provider, I want to feel confident my clients will be safe in their hands. It might sound overly protective, but my clients MATTER to me.

8 Ways to Mind Your Own Business

If their social media and website look good, be sure to get reference AND check them. This is not fool proof, but at least you have done what you can to protect yourself and clients.

Interviews and Hiring and Paperwork, Oh My

Traditional and contract employees work differently but they require the same process for onboarding. It starts with your due diligence.

I like to start my hiring process with some specific wording in the job posting I will use to attract new staff members. Here is a good example from a business I started and sold.

When I had my coffee shop, I placed a job posting for baristas. Since I was looking for quality over training, I mentioned training was provided. I also mentioned that they must love coffee, be a people person, and a morning person. Of course, I was very clear and asked for resumes and references, so I could look at work history.

I received many dozens of applications; it was almost overwhelming. Since I had requested a resume… anyone who did not provide one, didn't make the final cut or get an interview. It sounds harsh, but they didn't even follow the first set of directions I gave them.

When it was time to set up interviews for the top dozen or so applicants, I only offered early morning appointments. After all, I said they needed to be a morning person. Coffee shops open early, I was looking for someone who could open at 6 AM if necessary. If they can't make it to an early appointment, they are probably not a good fit.

When they arrived for their interview, I watched for signs. If they arrived late or looked like they just fell out of bed... warning sign. I offered them a coffee, latte, breve, or other yummy treat and watched for signs. A few even said they didn't drink coffee! Now I may not be the sharpest pencil in the box but REALLY? That was a warning sign.

After I had interviewed several potential employees, I checked their references! Looked at their social media profiles and talked to previous managers. Did I mention, you can learn a lot from a person's social media!

While it didn't really apply to my coffee shop staff, some industries really benefit by putting potential employees through assessments, to look for strengths and natural tendencies. Finding the right person for the position, and the company, is half the battle.

Finally, I hired a few people who seemed to be outgoing and pleasant. It takes time to do it right, but it pays off later. They don't all work out, that's to be expected, but I did find some amazing employees, because I was strategic about my hiring process.

It might sound like I went out of my way to trick my potential employees, but really, I was weeding out potential future problems in a gentle way.

8 Ways to Mind Your Own Business

Employee turnover is expensive! You will be spending your time reading the resume, interviewing the person, doing the hiring paperwork, training them, and more. In some industries, people don't last a week before they move on! That costs time and money.

Good employees are not always easy to find, and over the years I have learned some important lessons. Ask for resumes when you take applications, if they don't provide one, they must not be serious about the opportunity. Always check their references and social media accounts, you might be surprised by what you learn. Use psychometric assessments to better understand your potential employee before you hire them. To improve your chances of hiring well, I recommend you create a process to follow, and follow it every time! This ensures you are not discriminating against anyone… and creates beautiful records.

Training for Success

Once you have hired great people, now it's your job to keep them. I find the best way to keep good people is to equip them for success and be a good leader.

Statistics show that people are more content when working to their strengths. Not everyone is suited for every position, but that doesn't stop them from applying. You will be steps ahead knowing a potential employee is a good fit for the position before you hire them.

Well trained employees are more effective and more content, so be sure to offer adequate training. Don't assume they will pick up the skills they need to succeed, offer a systemized way to ensure everyone can be successful in their position.

A good leader will listen to their staff members and pay attention to the culture of the organization. They will care about their employee's wellbeing. Hear what they have to say about their work experience. Make it feel safe to have an opinion or an idea to improve something.

People who feel valued are happier in their work, and happy employees produce better results in your business.

Inspired Employee

The world has never needed inspired leaders like it does now. Leaders who have a deep understanding of themselves, including their intellect, their emotional intelligence, and their spiritual intelligence. The information Clara covered in the Matters chapters, has given you a solid foundation for you to make intelligent choices about building and growing your business. The work I have covered has been more focused on building the foundations of your emotional intelligence and self-image.

As your business grows you may reach a point where there is too much work for you to do, or you'd like your business to have access to some specialist expertise. This support can come in different forms. The traditional route is to hire an employee. You will need a clearly defined role, as well as having processes and procedures in place for managing them.

An alternative route, which is gaining popularity, is to out-source your needs to either a virtual assistant, or another company. This can be a great way to reduce costs and management responsibilities. You can set deadlines and expectations for outcomes but not dictate their schedule.

What is important for you, when taking on additional support, is to be able to effectively communicate your needs.

Communicating your Needs

When you aren't good at communicating your needs, it can lead to irritation, frustration, and even resentment. Being able to express yourself clearly and concisely is a valuable skill. So, I would like to ask you to think about your communication style. Do you feel like you could communicate more effectively? Do you ever feel irritated, annoyed, or frustrated by certain situations or people? Do your thoughts ever replay past events, replacing unwanted language and actions, with the ones you would have wanted them to be?

Chances are you may say YES to some, or all, of these questions.

The way you communicate can fall anywhere along a spectrum from passive to aggressive. Let's explore what these different forms of communication styles look like.

Passive communication can be where you don't feel comfortable speaking your mind, so your body language becomes closed off. You may fold your arms or sit with your legs crossed. You might be looking down and not maintaining eye contact. Your voice could be quiet, and the words you use could beat around the bush, leaving the other person unclear about what you are asking. Your energy, or connection, seems to lose strength and not reach the other person.

Maybe you say things like, "Um, I'd really like you to be able to… well, do you think you might, um… Don't you think it would be a really good idea if one of us went to that event on Friday? I was hoping you, um, might wanna, you know, stay here and…" I think you get my drift. There are a lot of words, but you don't effectively say, for example, you want someone to cover for you whilst you attend an event. All you are doing is hinting at what you want, which may leave the other person confused.

At the other end of the scale is an aggressive communication style. Here your words are strong and forceful. You may be critical, demanding, and even judgemental. The body language is different. You may lean forwards towards the other person, looking them right in the eye, maybe even with hands on hips. Your voice could be loud. The strength of your breath not only reaches the other person, but literally blasts them. You could say things like, "Look here, I'm going to that event next week whether you like it or not. So, I want you to look after the office and take care of everything." This has a really different feel than the passive approach.

Ideally you want to find a place in the middle of these two. A place where you communicate your needs effectively and say how you feel. For instance, "I'd really like to attend that event on Friday, as I feel it would be really beneficial to the business, and I would be grateful if you could take care of running the staff meeting for me. Would that work for you?" Notice how many 'I' statements there are. You expressed what you wanted. It is a much less stressful approach than the other two.

Life is like a mirror. What you give out, you get back. If you give out aggression, you are likely to have aggression reflected back at you. If you give a smile, you are likely to see a smile. If you communicate in a friendly assertive way, you are likely to get an honest response. This doesn't mean you'll always get what you ask for, rather you will feel less frustrated and stressed, because you have been able to communicate your needs.

Dealing with Difficult Conversations

When you start hiring other people, it will likely change the dynamics of your business. You may find yourself more open to new ideas and new ways of thinking. You might even feel the joy of sharing and building ideas with another. Having someone to bounce ideas off can be inspiring and take your product or service creation to the next level.

Even though working with others can bring much joy and expansion of thought, it can also have its difficulties. We all have our own perceptions, our own ideas of what is right or wrong. We all get hurt and upset for different reasons. In short, managing people or relationships, can be difficult at times. This can lead to situations where we may need to have a difficult conversation.

Having a conversation with someone else about their attitude, their standards of work, their lack of productivity, their pay, hours, behaviours, or anything else, can be tricky. If you know this is something you'll need to tackle, you can think about it in advance. You may imagine how the conversation will go. You might feel worried, concerned, anxious, and even fearful of the outcome. If you have ever experienced this, know that you are not alone. The majority of managers will have, at some point, dreaded having a difficult conversation with someone. You can put off the conversation, hoping things will sort themselves out, but usually they continue to deteriorate.

If you put off communicating, there is the potential to focus on the problem. You may feel a level of irritation, annoyance, or even anger building within you. Your emotions have the potential to become like a pressure cooker inside of you. At any moment, the lid can come off, and out will explode all the pent-up emotions you have been holding in.

As you can imagine this isn't a great idea. It certainly doesn't create great relationships moving forward. So, I would like to share with you a fantastic technique for dealing with difficult conversations. It is one I have used numerous times, in all sorts of situations, both personal and professional. I have shared it with my clients too, and they have reported great results using it. This only works when you know you need to have a difficult conversation.

Say you have appointed a virtual assistant from a different country to help with some of the paperwork and social media posts. At first the working relationship is great. You feel free to do the important and value-added tasks, whilst having let go of some of the things you weren't so keen on doing. It has been easier than taking on an employee.

Then one day you receive a message from a friend about one of your blog posts, saying she is surprised at the negative tone of it, for it doesn't sound like you. You feel puzzled and look at it. The wording is all wrong. The message isn't what you intended at all. Somehow your meaning has gotten lost in translation. This isn't good. You read some of the other posts your virtual assistant has made on your behalf, and you are dismayed. They aren't worded in the right way.

The comments people are leaving below the posts aren't great either. In fact, some of them are down-right awful. You are being accused of being disrespectful and rude. You don't know what to say. You think that maybe your assistant has just made a mistake. You wonder whether you should say something now or leave it and see what happens. Maybe you write a quick email asking your virtual assistant to follow your instructions. Then, you get on with your work and think that things will be ok.

Yet the errors in communication continue. The negative comments on social media are starting to affect business. Sales have taken a bit of a dip. You are being accused of behaving in a way you know you wouldn't. You know you need to have a proper conversation with this virtual assistant before it is too late. You want to reach out and contact them now, yet inside you can feel the swirl of emotions and you know as soon as you start talking to them, that the lid of the pressure cooker is likely to come off and you may say things which you later regret. You think they could be doing this on purpose, or being down-right sloppy with their work, or not checking what they are doing. But is this really true?

Instead of ringing or emailing that person right away you decide to sit down and do this exercise. Grabbing a notebook and pen you start by writing about the situation. You put down your understanding of what they should be doing in accordance with what they are being paid for. How you feel they are taking the copy you are supplying and changing the meaning of it. You write the implications of their actions and how this is making you feel. You keep writing until you feel you have put all the elements of the situation down.

Next you move on to writing what you want to say to them. Here you don't hold back. You put exactly what you want to say, even though you know in reality you wouldn't dare speak to someone like this. In this exercise you are as free to be an honest as you want, for they are never going to read it. In fact, no-one is ever going to read it. So, you can be true to how you feel. No holds barred, you put your feelings down on paper.

When you feel like you have said all you want to say, you pause for a moment and mentally put yourself in the shoes of the other person. Close your eyes and see yourself as them. Then when you feel ready to, begin to write from their perspective, responding to what you have said. As them, write what you intended to achieve with your actions. Write with no holds barred. Whatever comes to mind is right. Don't worry that you couldn't possibly know what is inside of another person's head, it doesn't matter. Just keep writing until you feel you have said all you can say in response to what you wrote to them.

Then once again pause for a moment. You may like to close your eyes again and mentally put yourself back in your own shoes. When you feel you have done this, pick up your pen and reply to what the other person said. Anything you write is ok. Write how you feel about their response and what you want to happen. Be clear. Get any last remnants of emotion out of your system.

Once you have done this, check how you feel. If you have given this exercise the proper focus and time, you should feel lighter. You can destroy what you have written during this exercise.

Now that you have levelled out your emotions, you are in a better place for having the actual conversation with the other person. Having written down what you want to say, and how you perceive they will respond, and what you want to say in return, you are now in a much more emotionally intelligent place to have the actual conversation.

Like most people who do this exercise, you may find the actual conversation is nothing like what you had thought it would be. Now that you aren't joining the conversation with heightened emotions, which is likely to create the same from the other person, you will find the conversation is more open. By doing this exercise you have opened your perception and your heart to making a connection with the other person. You are now more likely to find a win-win situation to moving forward.

This is a wonderful technique to do ahead of a difficult conversation, but what if it arises in the moment and you aren't able to plan for it! The first thing I suggest you do, as you listen to someone's unhappy perspective, is to take a deep breath. Practice breathing in for the count of four, holding for the count of four, releasing for the count of four, and holding out for the count of four. Keep repeating this as long as you need to. The other person will not know you are doing this as you listen to them.

As you listen, realise their words are their perspective. Angry words come from a place of hurt and fear. They are a reflection of who THEY are. Feel compassion for their pain, and do not take it personally. If you feel yourself wanting to react negatively, pause, take a breath, and let it go. Tell yourself you can handle any situation. That you can find a positive way forward. And know this to be your truth.

Once you feel calmer, you are now ready to handle the conversation.

For a one-off difficult conversation with someone, the above techniques are great. If conversations with the same person becomes problematic, a different approach may be required, and it may be a good idea to look at your boundaries. When we have good self-esteem and respect for ourselves, we set healthy boundaries regarding what situations we will allow into our lives. We may want to think about letting in the company of those whom we feel are life supportive and releasing the company of those who drain us of energy. We do not need to put up with someone else's bad behaviour

Building Great Relationships

Working with inspired people is all about building great relationships. With the previous exercise you looked at balancing your emotions ahead of having a difficult conversation. You also learnt in this chapter, how to communicate your needs. So, what other ways can you build great relationships with other people?

The first and most wonderful gift you can give to another person is to listen to them. We all want to be heard, yet so many of us don't participate in opening our heart and fully listening to another. Instead we allow our minds to be full of what we need to do next, or what we want to say next. When we interrupt, we are showing that we aren't fully interested in hearing what they have to say. When we aren't listened to, we don't feel valued.

Giving another person our time, where we fully participate in engaging in listening, can create huge benefits, both to ourselves and the business.

Realise that we bring our whole selves to work. When we have something going on within our personal life, it is difficult to leave that at home. So, feel compassionate for another. Realise we are all human, not machines. I have seen so many managers lead from a performance perspective only. I have experienced how it feels to be managed in this way, as well as witnessing it happening to others. It doesn't feel good.

When I managed staff, I opened my heart and mind to them. I gave them the space to talk about their personal issues. For instance, one day I realised that something was wrong with one of my members of staff. Her productivity was dropping off. She wasn't her usual light and bubbly self. She had lost a lot of weight. So, I called her into the office for a chat.

It can be difficult opening-up and talking to your boss, so I created a space of compassion, with no judgement, and I listened. I didn't expect her to open-up and tell me her problem if she didn't want to. But I did allow her the space to do so if she felt comfortable enough.

After the breakdown of her marriage she had fallen in love with someone and thought it was wrong. She was mentally beating herself up. At first, she didn't want to tell me, and I didn't push it. I just told her I was there for her. That I would help her in any way I could. That there was no right or wrong. I showed her compassion and would be there to listen to her with heart and mind if she ever wanted to talk.

When she did talk, I did as I promised, I listened to her with compassion. Her bravery was amazing, and it was a humbling experience to be part of that conversation. She told me she was afraid I would think less of her, but I certainly didn't. I gave her a hug and told her that we can't help who we fall in love with, and she should follow her heart.

She told me later that our conversation was a turning point for her. For it was shortly afterwards that she started telling colleagues about her new relationship. Feeling listened to had given her the courage to do what she felt was right. Not only did she blossom as a person after that talk, her productivity rose too. She became my most loyal member of staff. The day I told her I was moving on to another position she told me that I was the best boss she had ever had, and she would really miss me.

Working with others can be a wonderful experience. We can learn so much about ourselves in the process too. We can learn how our own perceptions aren't reality. We can learn that by giving of ourselves for a short period of time, we can create a big difference in the life of someone else.

When we get our ego out of the way, we become open and receptive to new ideas and new ways of working. We can even see how life mirrors back to us what we give out. This can lead to great change within us.

It can also inspire another on their life journey too. It can inspire them to step into their greatness. To be more loving, compassionate, and generous in their work. When we let go of struggle, and the need to be better than anyone else, we can build the most wonderful, supportive, loyal people around us. We certainly do get back what we give out.

8 Ways to Mind Your Own Business

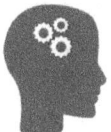 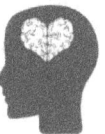

8 Inspired Ways that MATTER

We've covered a lot of topics in this book, hopefully you have taken the time to work through the exercises, we recommended along the way. If not, we encourage you to do so BEFORE launching your new business. As an added resource for your journey, we pulled all 8 topics into this final chapter.

Passion MATTERS

- Take time for self-discovery before starting your new journey into business ownership. Knowing how you prefer to work, and your natural strengths will help set you up for success.

- Give due diligence the attention it deserves, learn everything you can about the industry and new business you are considering. Knowing what you are getting yourself into before you start will save you valuable time and resources later.

- Plan, plan, and then plan some more. Create a strategic plan that clearly defines what your new business will look like some day, and all the steps necessary to get you there. Don't get stuck here; but do the work before you move on.

Inspired Passion

- Be clear about what you want, and mindful of what you believe you deserve. Your desires are powerful, but your beliefs are even more powerful. If left unchecked, you can end up self-sabotaging your success. Know that all is possible.

- Be clear of your intentions. How you want to BE as a person, which is your emotional intelligence, actions, and behaviours. And what you want to DO, the things you want to have and the experiences you want bring into your life and business. Allow your intentions to provide you with a balance across work, health, relationships, and financial prosperity. Then be sure that these intentions come from your heart and aren't there to satisfy the desires or wishes of someone else.

Creation MATTERS

- Get creative. This part should be fun, not stressful. Settling on a company name, logo, colors, and who you serve, is the foundation of your new business. If you struggle with this part find someone to help you brainstorm.

- Let your core values guide your decisions about the company culture you would like to create.

8 Ways to Mind Your Own Business

Doing this intentionally is much easier than trying to correct a problematic culture later.

- Get your goals out of your head and onto paper. Better yet, get them on a white board or poster board where you can see them every day. As you create your goals, pay attention, and see if they are SAVVY. Strategic, Actionable, Values Based, Visionary, You Focused goals.

Inspired Creation

- Remember that your intentions are like seeds. They are pure potential for growth and can blossom into reality. They need the right environment to flourish. Your doubts, concerns and worries, as well as those you hear from other people, are like weeds which come up and threaten to suffocate your growing seedlings of intention.

- Become consciously aware of your thoughts and feelings. If you feel good, it goes without saying that your thoughts must be good. If you aren't feeling so good, check into your feelings. Acknowledge them and see what you can learn from them. Then change your thoughts, realising that your thoughts are just thoughts, they aren't necessarily reality.

- Choose to use words which support and nourish the growth of your intentions. Release any words which aren't in alignments with them. Use supportive words to raise your belief in you, and what you can achieve. See your intentions playing out in your mind as if you have already realised them.

Business MATTERS

- It is always a good idea to talk to an accountant and tax attorney about your own situation, prior to making the decision about the structure of your new business. You could change it later if necessary but it's easier to do it right from the start.

- Licensing requirements are different based on your location. Check on the requirements at the national and local levels, to ensure compliance on your part.

- Be sure to protect all your assets; get the appropriate insurances and supplemental coverages for your family and new business. It will give you some peace of mind and protect you if something should happen.

Inspired Business

- Become the observer of your life and let go of any attachment for life to show up in the way you want it to. When you try to control life, it is a reflection that you aren't trusting and allowing. This may lead to feelings of resentment, irritation, frustration, and even anger that things aren't in alignment with your plan. Trust and know that taking inspired action will move you forward in the right way, at the right time.

- Allow yourself time to know and understand your actions, thoughts, and behaviours. Many of them are learnt responses which may or may not serve you. Unhelpful beliefs may get in your way of success and show up as self-sabotage. Your inspiration, or gut feeling, will always take you in the right direction. Listen to it and take action on it.

Operation MATTERS

- Find the tools you will need to create marketing materials and promote your new business. Some marketing tasks might be outsourced, but others will become ongoing activities within your operations plan.

- Get organized. The time to create systems, files, and forms, is BEFORE you need them. Over time you will no doubt create more of them but start with the basics. Make it a habit to create trackable and consistent operations as your business grows. If a task happens repeatedly, create a way to systemize it for consistency.

- Plan to show gratitude. You can feel grateful for your customers, but you must create tangible ways to SHOW your appreciation for those that make your success possible. Don't leave this to chance.

Inspired Operations

- Take regular time to step out of DOING mode. Although doing is good, it is easy to get caught up in doing something for the sake of it. Your ego may tell you to do more, to do it faster and better, and may keep on pushing you because it is never satisfied. Meditation, mindfulness and journaling all help to get you back into your intuition and take the inspired action which is right for you. When you take time out to really listen to YOU, you will find that you are productive in the right way.

- Use the power of your amazing imagination to visualise how you want your business to be. If seeing the big picture is difficult, envisage the next steps. Extend the practice of using your imagination from the point of view of others, like your customers and suppliers. It will help you to see whether there are improved ways of working with them.

- Consciously choose to use language which supports the achievement of your intentions. Use positive, active language as if what you want is already in existence. Then feel grateful for what is to come.

Prosperity MATTERS

- Use the value offer method when setting your pricing, the goal is to offer great value in your products or services, instead of racing to the bottom of the pricing barrel. You want to attract the right customers, not the bargain hunters.

- Your budget is just a matter of money in, and money out, for your new business. It is a dynamic tool which changes over time, and it will be critical as you experience the normal cycles of business.

- If you are not self-funding or bootstrapping your new business startup, your potential funding sources usually have a lengthy process that takes time. Plan accordingly.

Inspired Prosperity

- Money and wealth are not the same thing. You can have lots of money and feel poor, or have little money, and feel abundant. Feeling prosperous is a mind-set. Become good at giving AND receiving.

- Be clear on the distinction between what you WANT to happen, what you BELIEVE will happen, and what you EXPECT to happen. They may seem similar, but there is a real difference. Reach for a level of knowing and expectancy, that what you want will happen. Then when you meet a challenge along the way, your faith remains unwavering, and a way is found to overcome any situation.

- Gratitude is one of the greatest practices you can use. To feel grateful for what you already have, as well as what is yet to come, is a mark of trust that it will appear. Daily gratitude will allow you to be more aware of the things in your life and business to be thankful for.

Connection MATTERS

- Get comfortable with your two-minute commercial, a clear and concise definition of what you do will help you sound like the professional you are.

- Networking in your community will grow your customer base locally, decide which groups will give you exposure to your ideal customers. Then show up, speak up, and make a difference.

- Connecting with your potential customers online, will require consistency. There is a ton of "noise" to cut through, and your consistent and authentic interactions will make the difference.

Inspired Connections

- Connect with the wondrousness that is YOU through daily meditation, journaling, and spending time in silence. This will allow you to recharge your batteries. These practices not only help you to become more emotionally intelligent, they also enable you appreciate, like, and even love yourself more. Then you will hear your intuition, sense how much you can push yourself, and know when you need to

8 Ways to Mind Your Own Business

rest. When you are connected with yourself, you will better connect with others.

- Release the need to be all things to all people. You can't please everyone, be authentic to you. If you do things in order to win the approval of others, you will never find true happiness. When you find the confidence and belief within yourself to speak your truth, your tribe will find you.

- Use the power of story to really connect your message with others. Engage others with a story they can relate to, like how your product or service makes a difference. Dare to be creative with your communication and see a transformation in the level of engagement you experience.

Customer MATTERS

- Master the art of serving your customers. Go the extra mile and always be kind and compassionate. We all remember when someone makes us feel valued as a human.

- Work from a place of integrity, your customers will recognize it and reward you with loyalty. They are also more likely to refer you to a friend, knowing you will take good care of them, that is GOLD my friend!

- Remember your customers are your most valuable assets, in fact they pay the bills, find ways to show them how much you appreciate them.

Inspired Customers

- Check in with how you think and feel about your past, present, and future customers. Are you taking your current customers for granted, and only focused on gaining more? If you are focused on what you don't have, shift your focus onto what you DO have. Move your language and thinking from lack and limitation, to belief and expectancy of receiving what you want.

- Use the power of your imagination to reframe events or situations which did not happen as you would have liked. When you do this, it helps you to let go of unwanted thoughts, actions and behaviours, and re-programme your sub-conscious with the way you wished you had conducted yourself instead.

- Use your imagination to view your business from your customer's point of view. Think of all the different channels through which your customer comes into contact with you and envision that process. It will help you to create a great customer experience.

Employee MATTERS

- Consider all your options for extra help in your business, keeping in mind what you want your future business to look like. For many businesses, growth is still possible without the commitment of full-time employees.

- Have a systemized method for vetting and hiring employees, you are more likely to find the quality you are looking for, while avoiding inadvertent discrimination.

- Equip your interns, apprentices, contract workers, and employees, with the information and training they need to be successful. Be the kind of leader that makes them want to follow you!

Inspired Employees

- Pay attention to how you communicate your needs. Find a middle ground between being passive and aggressive. Then you can communicate your needs effectively and say how you feel.

- Balance your emotions prior to having a difficult conversation. Putting your thoughts, feelings, and what you want to say down on paper first, is a great way to get any frustration, irritation, and annoyance off your chest. Then destroy the paper. Your conversation will then be more balanced, and you will more likely find a win-win situation.

- Open yourself up to building great relationships with others. Practice listening with your whole heart and mind. We all want to feel heard, and when we do, we feel valued.

Conclusion

There you have it, 8 ways to mind your own business! In the creation of this book, every effort was made to inform and educate you about the basics of starting a new business, but we encourage you to continue learning. Each business adventure is different, don't be afraid to forge your own path, after all, you are the captain of this ship.

Thank you for giving us your time and attention, we trust you have enjoyed reading this book as much as WE have enjoyed writing it.

From that first idea you had about starting a new business, until the day you reach your dream, it is our sincere hope your new journey will be filled with personal fulfillment and prosperity.

 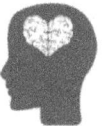

Inspired Afterword

You may have reached the end of the book, but really it is still the start of your journey. No matter how far along you now are in creating your business, the path ahead will continue opening out and the way will become clear. It is like taking a car journey. When we set off along the road you can only see the next 50 metres or so, yet you trust that as your foot stays steady on the gas, that the next part of the road will unfold before you as you move forward. This is the same with your business journey.

The one thing that can really get in your way are your levels of fear. We all experience fear at different levels. I know it has been a part of my own life, holding me back in so many ways. Yet fear doesn't need to hold you back. You can acknowledge fear and take it along on your journey. Show it the way. Soothe it and talk it out of existence, by acknowledging that you, rather than it, is the provider of your safety and security.

Fear stems from the ego. It will keep you within its learned limits and hold you small, if you let it. This is its security method. It is afraid that you will make some wrong turns and that you may get hurt. Now you know this, you can hold its hand and reassure it that you are able to create your own safety. That you know that what you are doing is the right thing.

Trust that your intuition is leading you in the right direction and dare to keep taking those steps forward.

About Clara Rose

At a relatively early age, Clara discovered an appreciation for the written and spoken word; it offered her an outlet for her creative side and outgoing personality. After college she worked in a variety of positions but found that in each position, she gravitated toward educating and leading others, finding her own fulfillment, in their success and professional development.

With a natural entrepreneurial spirit, Clara also discovered she had a passion for business development. Guiding an aspiring or new business owner on their journey, and giving them the necessary tools for success, brought her great satisfaction.

More than 30 years in the making, Clara has built a life-long career around training and educating professionals and entrepreneurs; about business and professional development, using the written and spoken word. Her mantra is, "I could do that!"

Clara Rose currently works with entrepreneurs and professionals, who want to craft their messaging and create influence, to generate more leads. *She believes success is a matter of influence, but influence is not accidental. It comes from the implementation of a sound strategy, with the correct resources and tools.*

Clara is the chief editor for RoseDale Publishing, a press mark that produces non-fiction books for influencers. She is also the creator of the Brainstorm & Blueprint Method, a proprietary process for creating a manuscript for publication.

Additionally, she is the creator of online training program Influence University and the founder of the Influence Builders movement; an online group for sharing knowledge, tips, and tools, for business and professional development.

Clara Rose is CEO of **Intentional Influence**, a consulting practice focused on writing, speaking, and leading, to help entrepreneurs strategically and intentionally cultivate influence.

For more information, you can contact Clara directly at Hello@ClaraRose.com.

ClaraRose.com (Learn More)

TheInfluenceMethod.com (Influence University)

BuildingYourInfluence.com (Her blog)

About Debbie Clement-Large

There is often a point in our journey through life where we become face to face with the question of *who we are,* and *why life is showing up the way it is?* This can happen at any stage of life, although a lot of people experience this during a time known as the 'mid-life crisis.'

For Debbie, this moment appeared in her life, in a big way, just after her fifteenth birthday. Although the moment seemed like a crisis, it was actually a catalyst for a huge opportunity for spiritual growth.

Three weeks to the day, after her fifteenth birthday, Debbie's dad passed, the result of an unexpected heart attack. Debbie found herself facing a change like no other. Her confidence and self-esteem shot to pieces; she struggled to find her way through this dark time.

Then, at nineteen, she chanced across some personal development books. At first, she resisted the call to read them, but they kept showing up in her life until eventually she opened one and started turning the pages. She became a closet personal development reader, her confidence and self-esteem slowly started to grow; leading her to 'tread the boards' on numerous theatre stages, where she met her husband.

The call to follow a career in psychology was strong at this time, yet still she turned her back on the call to adventure. Instead, she took up a career offered to her by her employer, to become a Chartered Management Accountant. Ignoring her intuition, Debbie embarked on a six-year journey of learning, eventually qualifying in 2003.

She worked as a Senior Accountant for many years, managing multi-million-pound budgets, and holistically coaching her staff. All the while she knew it was in the wrong career.

An opportunity to transition into a new career as a Business Analyst came along; and after another two years of training, she qualified. Working on small and multi-million-pound transformation and change programmes; she found that both the project team, and those facing change were not supported emotionally through the change process.

Becoming a corporate coach, she undertook Advanced Life Coach training, Stress Management training, Cognitive Behaviour Therapy training, Assertiveness Coach training, Mindfulness training and Meditation training. Debbie became a *Licensed Heal your Life* teacher based on the philosophy of Louise Hay.

The most in-depth training, and the one she says has been the most beneficial and rewarding, was her four-year study of Spiritual Psychology. Undertaking all this training, *felt like coming home.*

8 Ways to Mind Your Own Business

Debbie founded her international and award-winning coaching practice, Why Follow the Herd, in 2015. Since then she has coached internationally across the UK, the US, Canada, and France. She blends her mix of traditional coaching practices with spiritual psychology to really help people to know themselves on a deeper level, and to learn the tools to empower lasting change.

The individuals, entrepreneurs, and businesses she works with, are empowered to live and work in a whole-hearted way through one to one coaching, workshops, and online audio and video coaching programmes.

Additionally, she is the Business Lead for Health and Wellbeing, for The Federation of Small Businesses in the UK.

Debbie lives by the mantra; *it is never too late to change your life.* If she can, you can too.

For more information you can contact Debbie directly at debbie@whyfollowtheherd.com

Find out more at **WhyFollowTheHerd.com**